Both Ends of the Candle

ALFRED SHAUGHNESSY

Both Ends of the Candle

PETER OWEN · LONDON

ISBN 0 7206 0513 X

PETER OWEN LIMITED
73 Kenway Road London SW5 0RE

First British Commonwealth edition 1978
© 1978 Alfred Shaughnessy

Printed in Great Britain by
Daedalus Press Stoke Ferry King's Lynn Norfolk

To Jean with love

CONTENTS

Act One: Young Claret

Act Two: Old Brandy

ILLUSTRATIONS

ACT ONE

Young Claret

— ONE —

A Mongrel Is Born in Mayfair

During the Irish potato famine of 1845-9 a man with the common Irish name of Shaughnessy emigrated from Ashford, Co. Limerick to Milwaukee, Wisconsin, USA.

In the course of time, Shaughnessy, as have many Irish emigrants to America, became a patrolman and rose to the rank of Chief of Police in Milwaukee.

This man had two sons, the younger of whom, Thomas, got himself a job on the Chicago, Milwaukee and St Paul Railroad, married Elizabeth Nagel, daughter of another Irish immigrant family and soon went up to try his luck in Canada, where William van Horne was building the great railroad system across the Dominion from coast to coast. Thomas Shaughnessy became van Horne's right hand man and later succeeded him as President of the Canadian Pacific Railway Company. In 1916 Sir Thomas Shaughnessy was created a peer of the United Kingdom, with William Waldorf Astor the first American to sit in the House of Lords. His peerage was recommended by Mr Bonar Law and Mr Redmond, the Irish Nationalist leader. His sponsor, when he took his seat, was Lord Northcliffe, an old friend.

But the year 1916 also brought great sorrow to the family of Lord Shaughnessy of Montreal. His younger son, Alfred, was killed by a shell while serving with the 60th Canadian Battalion in France. He left a widow, Sarah, only daughter of Judge Bradford of Nashville, Tennessee and a descendant on her mother, Sarah Polk's side of two Democrat Presidents, James Knox Polk and Andrew Jackson. He also left two small children, Elizabeth and Thomas.

In May 1916, two months after Captain Shaughnessy's death

13

in the trenches, his widow was delivered of a third child, Alfred, at Bucklands Hotel, Brook Street, a select family hotel in Mayfair where she was waiting for her husband's next leave from the Front.

Shattered with grief, Sarah Shaughnessy sailed for the United States in the White Star liner, *Olympic* (a sister ship of the ill-starred *Titanic*), taking her new baby Alfred across the U-boat infested Atlantic to join her two other children in Nashville.

Now that I am born, I can take up the narrative in the first person and relate that my early childhood was spent travelling endlessly in trains between Montreal and Nashville, sometimes journeying in 'Killarney', my grandfather's private and presidential railroad car, which was tacked on to the trains for his or his family's use. I have a vague memory of the wail of the locomotive's whistle, the clanging cow-bell, the thrill of sitting in the observation car at the rear, watching the Canadian landscape recede as the train thundered along the rails.

Memories of America at that time are confined mainly to being sick in the elevator at Marshall Field's store in Chicago and nearly being left behind with my nurse on the station at Detroit.

Woodstock, my mother's home in the outskirts of Nashville, was a typical old Southern mansion with a verandah, white columns by the door and cotton fields all around. Grandmother Bradford, whom we called 'Gomo', had a large staff of Negro servants, all affectionate, pearly-toothed, ostensibly happy blacks. There was old Sam, the chauffeur; Ferguson, a bent and elderly Negro butler with white hair; Pearl, the cook, and our old coloured nanny. They were only a generation or so away from total slavery but later, when 'Gomo' died, the servants at Woodstock wept and wailed long into the night.

All the same they didn't 'live in'. Even Gomo's lady's maid, a coloured girl called Hannah, was quartered in the separate compound of staff dwellings some way from the house, a place which always seemed to be alive with piccaninnies and the sound of singing.

Between 1916 and 1921 my mother visited England quite often and sometimes rented houses for us to stay in. One of these was Pashasham Lodge near Leatherhead and Mama, leaving a nurse in charge of us, led a fairly busy social life in London, watched over by her two close friends, Lords Beaverbrook and Northcliffe. These trips to the UK were always undertaken in Canadian

Pacific boats, first in the modest tonnage liners *Montcalm* and *Montrose* and later in the *Duchess* boats. Much later in 1930 I crossed in the glorious all-white *Empress of Britain,* pride of the Canadian Pacific fleet and arguably the most elegant liner of her generation. As the family of the President, we were always met off the boat at Quebec or Southampton by smiling officials in bowler hats, who escorted us down special gangways and through the customs.

Mention of the CPR liner *Montrose* reminds me that in 1910 my father as a young man was returning in her from Europe and, as Sir Thomas's son, was invited to sit at the captain's table. This close contact with Captain Kendall resulted in an unexpected thrill at the end of the voyage. He had a ringside seat at the skipper's behest, when a Scotland Yard detective, posing as a pilot, boarded the *Montrose* as she hove to in the St Lawrence River, and arrested Dr Crippen and Ethel le Neve. My father saw them taken off the ship.

Mama used to recount this adventure of my father's every time we visited the Chamber of Horrors at Madame Tussaud's in later years and stood ghoulishly staring at the waxwork effigies of the little bespectacled doctor and his lady.

There is little doubt that Grandad Shaughnessy was a man of tremendous determination, energy and drive. He was also ruthless, a touch arrogant and something of a financial wizard. His employees were terrified of him.

My own memories of the old man are hazy. I can just remember a short man with a trim goatee beard, dressed in frock coat and billycock hat, lifting my brother Tom and me onto the footplate of a CPR locomotive in Windsor Station, Montreal; sitting on his knee and getting a puff of his cigar; and tea at the Shaughnessy residence in Dorchester Street, Montreal after a visit to the theatre to see Sir Harry Lauder, when Grandad, whose sight was failing, had to grope for the paste sandwiches on the tea table.

When he died in 1923 all the CPR trains throughout the Dominion stopped in their tracks for two minutes. A whole district of Vancouver bears his name. He was one of Canada's great men.

In 1917 on a visit to Government House, Ottawa, my mother had met and later fell in love with one of the Governor-General's young

ADCs, Captain Piers Walter Legh, second son of Lord Newton.

A year or so later Piers Legh left the Duke of Connaught's staff to accept an invitation from the young Prince of Wales, who was forming his first household, to become his equerry. Legh had met the Prince in the war, when he was on the staff of Lord Cavan, and the two men had 'hit it off'.

In November 1920, my mother married Captain Piers Legh at St Peter's, Eaton Square and so 'Joey' Legh (he was so nicknamed by his brother officers in the Grenadier Guards) became stepfather to my sister Betty, brother Tommy and me. He was the nearest thing possible to a real father and nobody could have taken a greater interest in or shown more affection towards a bunch of American/Canadian stepchildren than he.

Mama's wedding to Joey gave us our first glimpse of the Prince of Wales, for the young heir to the throne came breezing into the church early and was shown into the pew just in front of where we three children sat with a nurse, all primped up in little lawn coats and white socks, awaiting the arrival of the bride.

Mama was late and I can remember the Prince tugging anxiously at his tie, shooting his cuffs and looking round. Perhaps *he* was late for another engagement.

After the wedding we moved into a tall house in Norfolk Square, Paddington, in those days a fairly respectable neighbourhood; a staff of servants was engaged – butler, cook, footman, two house-maids, kitchen-maid and lady's maid – and this was our home for the next fifteen years.

The Prince of Wales used to come quite often to Norfolk Square, either to dinner-parties or for a whisky and soda with Joey after a game of golf. On the latter occasions, we would be rehearsed in the royal bow (Betty would practise her curtsey) up in the nursery and then troop down to the drawing-room armed by our govern-ess, Miss White, with a selection of our exercise books to show the royal guest how clever we were. The poor man, tired after a stren-uous game of golf, would be obliged to flip over the pages of our wretched books, crammed with badly done sums, illiterate essays and inaccurate history. All he could manage to say, as he turned the pages with simulated interest, was: 'Jolly good, you know, jolly good, you know.' For some time after, he became known to us as 'Jollygoodyeknow'.

We saw more of the Prince one particular summer holiday when an old friend of Mama's, Mrs Lionel Guest, lent us a house at Ferring-on-Sea in Sussex. Nearby was another house, rented for the summer holidays by Freda Dudley Ward for herself and her two pretty daughters, Penelope (now Lady Reed, widow of Sir Carol) and Angela (later Lady Laycock).

The Prince of Wales came down to stay with Freda quite a bit that summer and would go off with Joey to play at various neighbouring courses. On occasions Tom and I went along as extra caddies to help spot the balls that fell in the rough. On one of these outings the Prince fluffed a very simple approach shot at one hole and broke his wooden-shafted no. 6 iron (mashie-niblick in those days) right across his knee, flung it away and swore he'd give up the game. I remember that my brother and I were rather shocked at this outburst of temper – on the golf course, too!

Leaving the Littlehampton Golf Club after one of those games, the Club Secretary came up to see us off as we climbed into the red-lined royal car with the Prince's chauffeur, Wagstaffe, at the wheel. A bit confused and not quite knowing how to address the heir to the throne, the Club Secretary said, extending his hand: 'Well, er, goodbye, er, Prince of Wales.' Tom and I knew *that* couldn't be right.

Whenever the Prince came to dine or to a party at 43 Norfolk Square, we could see from our nursery window a little knot of curious onlookers gathered on the pavement outside our front door, the red carpet across the pavement and the policeman on duty by the door. When the Prince's car arrived to mild cheering, we would creep down to the bedroom landing and peer over the banisters down into the hall to watch his arrival in the house. The servants were always on their best behaviour for these occasions, and the tension in the kitchen and pantry could be felt for days beforehand.

These experiences served me well in 1972, when writing the episode of the TV series *Upstairs, Downstairs* in which the Bellamy household at Eaton Place were similarly on edge before the arrival of King Edward VII to dinner in their house.

In 1924 my mother and Joey were blessed with a daughter, who was born at Norfolk Square, soon after Tommy went away to his first boarding school. I was sent off to the seaside with our governess, Miss White, to get me out of the way during Mama's confinement. The following letter I wrote at the age of eight in a childish scrawl to my mother on the subject of names for my new half-sister shows a distinct lack of taste and a scant knowledge of the facts of life:

> Dear Mummy, I hear a new baby has been born. I suppose we have to name her here goes: Mary, Isobel, Jane-Jane our stranger – Pauline, Jean, Ann, oh dear we shall have to search the 'dictionary'. Bye the bye where was she born, under your bed? please tell. There are a few Primroses in the garden and I will send you some if possible. I must close now because we are going out. Much Love from Frowner Freak.

I should explain that my mother nicknamed me 'Freddy Frowner' due to a nervous habit I developed as a child of screwing up my brow. 'Freddy Freak' was a kind of alliterative alternative. I always hated my two official Christian names, Alfred and James, which were both, as I told my mother later at the snobbish age of twelve, footmen's names.

However, as my father had been Alfred and known to everyone as Fred, I became Freddy, which I abhor. If ever a name conjured up a sort of P. G. Wodehouse, chinless, monocled idiot! The Hon. Freddy Threepwood, etc. But there was nothing I could do about it, so I've had to bear it throughout my life.

It was not long before our governess, Miss White, left us, for it was my turn now to go away to boarding school. And into No. 43 Norfolk Square came a woman of very special significance as nanny to little Miss Legh.

My half-sister was eventually christened Diana, and among her godparents were the Prince of Wales and the Admiral of the Fleet, Earl Beatty.

Diana's nanny, who also gave a hand with us during the holidays, was the nearest thing to a saint you could find outside the walls of a convent. Had she taken the veil and later qualified for canonization, the Devil's Advocate would have been hard pushed to find a single flaw in her absolute and total goodness.

When she died at her home in Hertfordshire aged eighty-two, some fifty or sixty members of the half-dozen families she had served in her lifetime came together from all over the world to pay their last respects to a great old lady. It was a tribute to her love of and devotion to her charges that in a working lifespan of sixty years, she had served so few families, remaining with each one for many years. She would only leave a family when the children were all teenaged and away at boarding schools, moving on to start again with a new baby or babies somewhere else.

At around seventy, when Diana was old enough for a governess, she retired from permanent nannyhood and embarked on a long period of temporary work, returning to many of the families to cope with holidays, weddings, christenings, the packing of school trunks and times of crisis. Like so many women who have dedicated their lives to what she herself would have called 'the nicer families' – by which she meant, of course, the titled upper-crust – our Nanny was a walking copy of *Debrett,* a mine of useless information as to the lineages and relationships of everyone in so-called 'society'.

My earliest and fondest memory of this dear old lady in tweed skirt and white blouse, her hair scraped back in a bun, wearing steel-rimmed glasses, is seeing her seated night after night at the nursery table after the nurserymaid had removed her supper tray; under the ceiling light she would sit with last week's *Tatler* (finished with downstairs) spread open before her. With a magnifying glass in her hand, she would pore over the photographs contained therein of society people at hunt-balls, point-to-points, shoots, meets, at Ciro's and on the racecourse. And she would mutter to herself, as the pages flipped over, 'Ah, there's that Stuart-Wills girl, the youngest; she married a Pelham-Smith, didn't she? Of course her grandmother on her father's side was a Monkton, such a lovely woman when she was a girl. The other daughter was the second Countess of Wanborough, with those two little boys, Jeremy and David. I packed both their school trunks. Jeremy's done so well, he's an ambassador now and David inherited Mallion Park . . . what a pretty picture of the Duchess of York and there's Miss Elizabeth at the races, always knew she'd grow into a beauty, she's got a look of her aunt, Lady Sheraton. . . .'

Some people find it hard to recall the actual names of their old nannies. 'Nanny' was just 'Nanny'. Not a person but an institution. For some reason we can all remember our nanny's name – three names, in fact, engraved forever on our hearts – Gertrude Alice Turnbull.

— TWO —

A Costly Education

In my minor years I attended three schools, all private, fee-paying and totally privileged. My first was a day pre-preparatory establishment in what was then Cambridge Street, W.2. (now Kendal Street) off the Edgware Road, run by a Miss Alexander. We were all nasty little six- to seven-year-olds, dressed in shorts, blazers and flat caps with a button on top, as we chattered and punched our way down Albion Street in a crocodile to play primitive cricket among the sheep in Hyde Park. I suppose I must have learnt something there, as my next place of instruction was Summer Fields, Oxford, a very well-known, highly scholastic boarding prep school that has turned out all sorts of celebrities ranging from Harold Macmillan and Lord Wavell to Julians Slade and Amery, Christopher Lee of 'Dracula' fame, the artist Victor Pasmore, and Lord Caccia, later our ambassador in Washington.

When I started there in 1925, Summer Fields had the reputation of winning most of the major scholarships for Eton, Harrow, Winchester and other leading public schools. The teaching, particularly of the classics, was superb. Among the staff there in my day were L. A. G. Strong, the novelist, who taught us French, and Cecil Day Lewis, who made our Latin periods pure joy by declaiming the speeches of Cicero with histrionic power and much swishing of his gown as though he was toga-ed in the Forum.

Summer Fields was a pretty tough and spartan school but for some reason I was immensely happy there. In the school plays staged in the gymnasium, I was always cast in the old men roles. One such was Old Gobbo in *The Merchant of Venice* in December 1927, when I was eleven. I wore a very long beard and played the part with a heavy stoop and a sort of husky whisper, which the

20

school mag's critic described as 'penetrating'. The faded programme in my scrapbook tells me that the Nerissa was Nigel
Nicolson, younger son of Harold Nicolson and Vita Sackville-
West, and the Prince of Arragon was G. K. N. Trevaskis (later Sir
Kennedy, the British High Commissioner for Aden and Southern
Arabia). He was known as 'Sus', Latin for pig, a term of endear-
ment really, for his collars were always grubby and his shirt tails
were invariably hanging outside his trousers. He was a very fast
bowler and highly popular. I also played Peter Quince in *The
Dream* on a lawn at Summer Fields one summer, using the same
stoop and penetrating whisper as for Old Gobbo. But a stiff breeze
minimized the effect and I wasn't mentioned in the review.

In the 'twenties many assistant-masters at prep schools had
recently fought in the trenches; some had been shell-shocked or
gassed and this apparently sanctioned a great deal of sadistic hair-
pulling, ear-twisting, caning and even punching of their pupils, if
Latin verbs were incorrectly conjugated or geometrical theorems
misunderstood.

I know I suffered a great deal of violence at the hands of some
of the crueller masters at Summer Fields, assaults which today
would land any teacher in a police court and on the front page of
The News of the World. But in those days one accepted the indignity of the outstretched hand or proffered bottom, the swish of
the cane, the sharp sting like a bread knife cutting through flesh.
Afterwards came the furtive reunion in the lav with a group of
curious, morbidly interested friends eager to inspect one's weals.

My views on corporal punishment are quite clear. I believe that
like TV violence, such practices can only harm disturbed boys with
inner problems, unhappy homes, a lack of love or of confidence or
those burdened with some handicap. A happy, integrated boy
from a good home can see all the bloodshed he likes on TV *and*
be caned at school without becoming a psychopathic killer. The
now defunct caning and fagging system in English schools could be
and, I suppose, was on occasions abused by a minute section of
vicious boys, if not properly supervised by lazy or careless house-
masters. But I still maintain, from my own personal experience,
that to be caned justly as a small boy was quite good for the soul; it
taught humility and it got the punishment over swiftly and sum-
marily, demanding guts and a bit of physical pain-endurance, two
useful qualities for later life. Better a quick beating and go free but

sore than spend a hot summer afternoon in a classroom re-writing Latin prose to the distant click of bat and ball.

I adored Eton, naturally, because I had athletic success there, which was paramount. I was captain of my Junior House Cricket XI, and ended up as Captain of my House, a member of 'Pop', Second Keeper of the Field and a school blue for boxing (middle-weight) and athletics.

In my second year I was also the Junior Victor Ludorum, which meant that in the Junior Athletics I won more points than anyone else. I was 14th in the steeplechase, 4th in the mile, 2nd in the half-mile, 1st in the quarter mile, 2nd in the 100 yards, 2nd in the hurdles, etc. and thus a sort of overall champion. I loved the sound of the title. Victor Ludorum. It conjured up a romantic vision of cheering crowds in the Colosseum, throwing flowers and garlands at me, as I was borne on a litter by Nubian slaves to be crowned by the Roman Emperor with a wreath of laurels, an object of envy for all my rival athletes and one of adoration and desire for the Vestal Virgins and other ladies present.

In the event, I received a credit at the School Stores for fifteen shillings and bought a pewter mug with my initials on it, which I promptly lost during a move to another room in my tutors'. But it still sounds good to me and the Latin words will always ring in my ears: Junior Conqueror of the Games. Yes, sir.

Although, following my brother's footsteps, I actually won a scholarship to Eton, it was only the nineteenth (out of some forty entrants) and so I was not elected to College. This meant that I automatically 'took Remove' and started off in the highest division of the Lower School with all the new collegers and 'Remove takers'. After this it seems, from reading my old reports, my work deteriorated. However, games and character seemed to matter most in those days and I somehow got through.

One intellectual activity that interested me very much at Eton was my membership of the Eton College Political Society, a small élite group of senior boys who met monthly in the Vice-Provost's study to be addressed by guest speakers of note, anxious to influence Etonian opinion. During my time we were visited by such varied orators as the Prince of Wales, Mr Reginald McKenna, Mr Gandhi and Sir Oswald Mosley, a good bag for one year. When Mosley concluded his address to us and asked for questions, my contemporary, Michael Astor, rose to his feet, every inch his mother's son, and asked politely: 'Could you tell us, Sir Oswald, who is to succeed you as leader of the British Fascists after you've been assassinated?'

It was a couple of seconds before Mosley collected himself and managed a somewhat hollow laugh. Boys will be boys.

After I'd taken School Certificate and become a modern language specialist, my academic life at Eton improved no end. With the early advantage of a strict French governess behind me, whose insistence on a correct accent had survived the usual mockery at school, I sailed ahead and became a good linguist in French and German. We acted plays in French, translated murder cases from German newspapers and held debates and mock trials in one or other of the studied languages. I found at last a subject that totally absorbed me.

When in 1934 my last year at Eton came along, it had already been decreed that I should go on to the Royal Military College, Sandhurst to train for a commission in the Grenadier Guards. Most of my friends were sweating their guts out with desperately difficult exams for the Foreign Office, for the Universities, or for Dartmouth and Cranwell. My lot was to sit for the Army Exam, universally known as the 'idiot's exam'.

Administered by the Civil Service, this absurd set of examination papers was about as easy as Common Entrance: simple maths, English, history, and so on. After the written part, provided he could spell his name and knew the French for a dog, a candidate had to present himself for an oral exam by the Civil Service Commissioners at Burlington House. Here you marched in and were asked a handful of simple questions like 'Why do you want to be a soldier?' and 'What are your favourite games?' They really wanted to make sure your neck was clean and that you could tie your tie, speak proper English and looked something like a human being. Any fool could pass the Army Exam and I did, early in my last summer half. So I spent a wonderful June and July riding all over Berks and Bucks on a bike which my house tutor, dear old 'Cyrus' Kerry, allowed me as a favour. I went racing and swimming at roadhouses as far away as Beaconsfield; I did no work; I played no cricket but frittered away the summer to get up steam for the gruelling first term that awaited me at Sandhust in the autumn.

— THREE —

Officer Material or What?

I may be the only individual in British history to be sent to Sandhurst twice. But that is another story. I am concerned here with the first time I entered that rigidly traditional, strictly military establishment as a gentleman cadet (imagine such a term today) in the autumn of 1934 to undertake the eighteen-month-long, three-term course for officers in the army.

Apart from the normal subjects officer cadets were taught quite a lot about constitutional history, the parliamentary system, economics and such like. There was a great deal of military history in the curriculum, regimental customs, origins of . . . , how Marlborough disposed of his infantry at Oudenarde, etc. Sandtables were studied of all the major battles since Hastings. Then there were the outside subjects, including much foot drill, weapon training, tactics, map-reading, PT and equitation, which was a polite term for learning to ride a horse.

After the lazy comfort of Eton it was a shock to have your hair cropped like a skinhead, to jump out of bed to a bugle-call at seven a.m. and parade in the half-light before a cadet-officer, who shone a torch on your chin to see if you'd shaved properly. In addition to all that, you were chased about up and down corridors, bawled at by Guards drill sergeants and senior cadets alike and frankly treated with great indignity. Punishments were frequent and severe during your junior term. For a Sam Browne belt or bayonet scabbard that wasn't waxed and polished like a mirror you could get three extra drills and spend Saturday afternoon in full marching order with pack being chased all over the square by a drill pig.

As everything at Sandhurst was alphabetical and my name began S-H-A I roomed and stood on parade and messed next to

Richard Sharples, whose name had always just preceded mine at Eton when 'Absence' was called.

Thus did Dickie Sharples and I share a 'kit' of specially polished bayonet scabbard, Sam Browne belt and spotless rifle for those dreaded kit inspections, when the junior under officer came round the rooms. One of us would show up the special kit for inspection, then, before the JUO stepped next door, a diversion was created taking his attention to the room he had just left on the other side of the passage. At this point the special kit was smuggled into the next room and as quick as a flash laid out on the bed in time to be inspected all over again.

I remembered this and other Sandhurst larks with a heavy heart when Dickie Sharples was brutally murdered with his ADC as Governor of Bermuda in 1974. His impish, mischievous chuckle and lovely sense of fun helped both of us to survive the horrors of that first term at the RMC in 1935.

For PT we had to parade in white flannels and blazers like chorus boys in a musical comedy with a ghastly red and white striped sort of bellhop's pill-box cap perched on our shaven heads, a relic of Queen Victoria's army. Equitation mornings were a special bind, for it was necessary to get up first thing for shaving parade in riding breeches, gaiters and boots, which took time to put on. The troop horses upon whose backs we jumped fences without saddles in the indoor riding school and scrambled and slithered up and down impossible sandy banks, were very varied in temperament and age. Some of them were old and tired and needed constant spurring to get them even to trot. Others – the ones I always seemed to get – were young, fresh and bloody-minded.

We were instructed in the art of riding by corporal-majors and corporals-of-horse of the Household Cavalry, so it was all strict ceremonial cavalry drill: 'Prepare to Mount.' 'Mount.' 'Walk March.' 'Trot.' 'Canter.' 'Gallop.' 'Charge.'

There were misty mornings out on the heathland round Camberley, when one could just believe one was at Balaclava with a cavalry horse between one's legs, thundering across the turf in line with a dozen others, letting out bloodthirsty cries like the Comanches in a western movie.

Before I went to Sandhurst I had only ridden small ponies as a child and donkeys on the beach at Margate. After a term at the

RMC I was quite proficient in the saddle and started hunting with the Garth and the Staff College Drag. I even grew so bold as to enter for the famous GCs' Race at the Garth Hunt Point-to-Point, an annual cavalry charge of some fifty cadets mounted on every sort of animal from hired cobs to well-bred hunters.

I hired a nag from a well-known horse-coper in Camberley, who assured me the beast was a good ride, knew the course and had taken part in the race for many years. The poor old thing was so unfit that he blew up half-way round the course and I had to pull him up. Just as well, perhaps, as we had hit every fence so far and it was only a matter of time before we finally came to grief.

After my junior term, I was told by my company commander that I was considered good officer material and would be promoted 'off the square', which meant that for my intermediate term I would be a corporal with some authority over others as a section-commander.

I was very bucked at this news and even more so when I was also appointed one of the select few of fellow intermediate corporals who were to be commandant's orderlies for the term. This meant that, on a roster, two of us had to go to the commandant's residence, Government House, to breakfast with him on Sunday morning and afterwards, dressed in church parade order with a special white buckskin belt-pouch and a silver-knobbed cane, to march up beside the general on to the saluting base and stand there, while he took the parade and ordered the march-off to the Sandhurst chapel.

It was quite an honour but an ordeal too. The trick was for the two orderlies to halt together on the saluting base exactly in step with the general and on the right spot. This required every single pace from the march-off outside Government House to the saluting base to be counted and the spot to halt on recognized by a patch of oil on the tarmac or some other pre-reconnoitred mark.

General Bertie Fisher, an old 17/21st Lancer, who'd soldiered with Haig, was my commandant. He was a charming man, but somehow a good breakfast in his house was always marred by the dread of not hitting that patch of oil or losing count of the steps. In the end my colleague and I managed it all right. On the silver tops of the orderlies' canes are engraved the names of past commandant's orderlies at the RMC, Sandhurst. I noticed on mine the name of David Niven, whom I was later to know. I've always meant to ask him if he ever missed the oil patch or lost count of the steps.

As a Roman Catholic I was obliged to attend evening Mass on the Sundays when I was commandant's orderly. But on other Sunday mornings at Sandhurst, when not on that duty, we Roman Catholic cadets were submitted to a hilarious, farcical performance: one of those special privileges – if you like – that RCs enjoy at Church of England schools. As a strange and curious minority sect of some twenty cadets, we fell in at church parade on the extreme left of the line, the whole RMC being paraded as a battalion of four companies.

After the inspection, the adjutant of Sandhurst, mounted on a fine horse, gave the command: 'Move to the right in fours, form fours, right.' Whereupon the whole parade obediently and with a crash of feet turned right. But the twenty cadets on the left of the line were seen to turn smartly, and as one man, to the left. There always followed a ripple of laughter which floated across the green lawn in front of the Old Building Parade Ground. This came from the sundry cadets' relations and guests, who had come to watch the parade. They believed that we had misheard the command, so far were we down the line. But it was quite intentional. More laughter was to come. The adjutant then gave: 'By the right, quick march.' The band struck up 'The British Grenadiers' or some suitable quick march and, as the whole RMC marched one way, we marched in the opposite direction, detaching ourselves from the main body like some guard's van that has come uncoupled from a long goods train.

Boldly, proudly even, for it was fun to hear the laughter, we marched on a matter of fifty paces or so to a point where twenty bicycles lay against a wall. These were ours and we grabbed them, mounting correctly in the proper cycle-drill manner under our senior cadet . . . 'Walk march, prepare to mount . . . mount,' but we were a tinny, scraping squad of clapped-out old second-hand bikes not a squadron of cavalry. Thus we rode in minority Papal pride and triumph to a tin shack in the back streets of Camberley, where a frail old priest mumbled Holy Mass.

There were some memorably happy days at the RMC as well as many grim ones. Of course, the June Ball was the climax of the year. You had your best girl down and there were fireworks, boating on and inundation in the lake, a band on the lawn, coloured lights – all the military splendour of an Indian Station in Victorian times.

You felt quite smart, if a little throttled, in your mess kit with its high collar and tight tunic with red on your navy blue epaulettes if you were, like me, a corporal. And you waltzed stiffly erect but with a sense of old-world romance.

I became so damn military during the start of my second term at Sandhurst that I grew a moustache and began to read regimental histories in the library. But then something began to happen to me. As the term wore on, I started to realize that I was studying the science of the slaughter of my fellow human beings. Suddenly the enormity of my chosen career clicked in my brain. What a wasteful life, learning to fire guns at men . . . preparing for genocide, waiting and hoping for a war in which to justify my whole education. Was this my vocation?

Towards the end of the term I knew I must do something quickly, if I was not to return to the RMC for my third and final term, when I would possibly become a junior under officer. I took a deep breath and marched myself in to see General Bertie Fisher. He was quite wonderful. I told him my feelings, honestly and in some detail. He was at first amazed, then sad and disappointed, but never angry. He asked me to think carefully for a while longer but I was determined to get out. I resigned the course and my resignation was accepted.

The wrath I really feared was that of Joey and indirectly of Mama. Again, to my joy and relief, they were both quite extraordinarily understanding and sympathetic. I think too they had begun to realize that an officer of the Grenadier Guards in 1935 needed considerable private means to live anywhere near up to the standard required. It was pointless to join the Brigade of Guards without owning at least half a dozen polo ponies, a couple of hunters and probably an aeroplane. The life of pleasure punctuated by short spells of soldiering was really for rich young men with nothing better to do. It was not for me and my parents knew it.

So I left the RMC behind me with just a tinge of regret. I'd made many good friends there and had a lot of fun. If I'd stayed on I might have been an under officer or even won the Sword of Honour but I somehow doubt it. I little realized as I drove through the Staff College gate into the Camberley High Street and away to London that within five years I was to go rocketing back into the damn place under very different circumstances and in a very different frame of mind.

— FOUR —

Dividends and Debutantes

I was now an ex-cadet, aged nineteen, and efforts were made and strings were pulled to find suitable employment for me whereby I might earn my living.

I had a narrow escape from banishment to India, when a kind man called Sir Percy Newsom, head of Jardine Matheson, the trading company, offered me a job in Calcutta. The salary was terrific, £500 a year, but I didn't fancy sweating it out in the Far East until my liver gave out, so I declined with gratitude.

It was an old family friend, Colonel Johnny Dodge, who finally came up with a job for me in the prosperous City stockbroking firm of Nathan and Rosselli, of which he was a senior partner.

Being an idiot with figures and lacking any ambition for a career in finance, I was soon bored stiff. My task was first to learn stockbroking as a trade, which meant scurrying about through the alleys and sidestreets of the City delivering contract notes, bearer bonds and God knows what to Messrs Guggenheim and Oppenheim, Sacker and Finsberg, Aaron and Isaacs and occasionally the Bank of England. It was nearer to a taxi-driver's training than a broker's. And second, to introduce new clients to Nathan's and earn myself commission on their business. The art of persuading people to part with their money – even in exchange for good shares – has always eluded me. I was a useless tout.

Desperate to overcome this ineptitude, I used to draw up my chair to rich friends at dinner-parties after the ladies had left the dining-room, take a deep breath and a swig of port and hear myself nervously saying: 'I say Eddie, have you got any Consolidated Metal Ordinary; if not, would you like me to buy you some tomorrow morning? They say there's a dividend increase on the

30

way.'

The conversation would usually end with Eddie selling me a car instead or landing me with taking his plain sister to a ball.

However, my time at Nathan's was alleviated more than somewhat by a friendship I struck up there with a young fellow-clerk called Philip Zorab. As I was only with the firm for a year and didn't come across Philip during my first four months there, I only knew him for a comparatively short time. He was, in fact, a 'blue button', which for those unversed in the ways of Throgmorton Street, means a specially-trained clerk, who dives in and out of the 'house' taking messages from his firm to the partners and dealers on the Stock Exchange floor.

What was more important to me was that he loved music, liked me and seemed to want a friend of his own age in the firm. We drifted together naturally, having that much in common. I liked and respected him very much, for he was brilliantly clever at finance and taught me a lot about money matters during our many lunches together at various city taverns up the narrow alleys off Moorgate and Threadneedle Street. We used to go to quite a few concerts together at the Albert Hall or the Wigmore Hall and once or twice, in the cheap seats, to the theatre and the opera.

I only visited his home once, for dinner one winter evening in 1936. We were demolishing a treacle pudding in the Zorab diningroom at their house on the edge of the Addington Golf Course near Sydenham and I was attempting to converse knowledgeably with Mrs Zorab about the symphonies of Bruckner, when the parlour maid entered swiftly and unexpectedly from behind a screen and said: 'Oh, madam, the Crystal Palace is on fire.' And it was. And there we were, eating treacle pudding within a few minutes' walk of the place. So dinner petered out, we grabbed coats, scarves and torches and hurried out to the blazing inferno. It was sad and rather grim to see that great Victorian greenhouse crashing down in a molten sea of twisted girders and blazing timber. There were literally hundreds of fire engines there. But nothing could save the Crystal Palace. And it was my friendship with Philip Zorab that has enabled me to record an eyewitness account of that particular moment in London's history.

Watching the flames leaping in the dark that night, Philip and I discussed, suitably, Wagner, *The Ring* and specifically *The Valkyrie*. Ironically, as a young Jew in 1936, he adored Wagner.

If Philip Zorab is still alive and happens to read this, I want to thank him and his mother for that dinner that was interrupted so dramatically that I forgot to at the time. This must be my bread-and-butter letter to them, forty years late.

Another friend I made at Nathan's was an ex-RAF officer called Sir Richard Barlow. Like me, he was on half-commission and in the spring of 1937 we were sharing an office.

Dick Barlow had a girlfriend in Copenhagen and wishing to visit her, persuaded me to share the charter of an aeroplane and fly there with him for the weekend. I jumped at it and we hired a Tiger Moth from a firm at Heston. We set out one morning in good weather to reach Schipol, Amsterdam for lunch and, hopefully, Copenhagen by dusk.

Unfortunately, having only a compass and a quarter-inch map for navigation, we drifted slightly off course and losing ourselves over the Baltic Sea, we finally had to make, unheralded, for Hamburg. Here the Nazi aerodrome officials were bloody-minded and suspicious. A lone English light aircraft coming in unannounced convinced them we were spies. Thus we were halted out on the field, some way from the tarmac, by customs men in a police car; the aircraft was searched, every leather cushion was thrown out on to the grass, our luggage was opened and we were questioned rather impolitely.

Having finally explained our unscheduled arrival at Hamburg and received permission to stay overnight, we parked the Tiger Moth and took a tram for the city in search of a hotel for the night. It was on this tram ride that I had my first glimpse of Nazi bestiality. Some SA Brownshirts were throwing an elderly Jewish couple off a tram on the other line; the man had fallen on to the pavement and he was being kicked in the face. The Hamburgers were walking past, averting their eyes, looking into shop windows and generally pretending that it wasn't happening. I had a job to restrain Dick, who was a hot-tempered fellow, from jumping off our tram to intervene. I'm a bit ashamed to say I funked it. And that is roughly the story of the Third Reich. People funked it, didn't want a bayonet in their guts, and said nothing. Like me.

The next morning we took off from Germany with some relief and the contrast with Hamburg – all uniformed officials and fighter planes across the other side of the aerodrome – was striking when later on we touched down in a dandelion field with a windsock and a few wooden huts, where a man came out to us as we taxied in, raised his soft felt hat and said, 'Good morning, welcome to Denmark.'

On the way home we avoided Hamburg like the plague but half-way across the Baltic we spotted a warship below, cruising in the sun surrounded by small craft. Going down to 700 feet, we were able to identify the German pocket battleship *Admiral Scheer* escorted by a flotilla of U-boats. As we flew over the funnels of the *Admiral Scheer* I slid open my window and took a snap of it with my VPK, which came out, alas, as a meaningless blur. A month later, Dick, in whose name our plane had been chartered and its papers made out, received a tongue-in-cheek rebuke from the Civil Air Authority. The *Scheer* had taken our number and reported us. We were probably quite lucky not to be shot down.

From 1935, when I left Sandhurst, up to the outbreak of war in 1939 I really lived the social round to the full. Most of my even-ings and weekends were spent at dinner-parties, private or charity dances, some grand balls and an endless tour of shooting parties and summer weekends as a guest at one or other of the stately homes of England.

My indirect connection – through Joey – with Court circles caused me to be placed on all the hostesses' lists as an eligible young man available for pre-dance dinner-parties in the London season. And so, night after night through the heat of May and June, I would set out in my little Wolseley Hornet dressed up in white tie, boiled shirt and tails for some elegant house in Mayfair or Bel-gravia there to dine with people I'd never set eyes on before. On one occasion, when there were two deb dances on the same night in Belgrave Square, I went on from my dinner-party to the wrong dance and spent two hours drinking champagne to which I was not entitled.

The world in those days seemed to be filled with lovely, fresh and exquisitely dressed young women to sit next to at dinner, dance with, punt on the river with, go racing with, take to the theatre and the opera and sometimes, with a bit of luck, lure on from a deb dance to the Coconut Grove or the Florida, later to kiss awkwardly in the back of a taxi speeding round Marble Arch or Hyde Park Corner on the way home to Mummy.

1936 was a vintage year for girls: Mary Malcolm, Antonia Snagge, Rose Paget, the Kenyon-Slaney sisters, the three lovely

Wyndham-Quin daughters, the Lloyd-Thomas girls, Pam, Cissie and Anne, Jean Ogilvie, Irene Haig and, perhaps the dishiest of them all, Zara Mainwaring.

There can be no doubt that Zara was the prettiest girl I ever saw. She had fair curly hair, pale blue eyes, a lovely little nose and a slight dimple. She was breathtaking.

Once at a young peoples' dinner-party before some deb dance at which Zara was a guest, our host, an ageing peer of whom we young men were in some awe, rose as the ladies left the dining-room, closed the door and ordered us to charge our glasses. Believing he was about to propose a toast to his good wife, who had fed us all excellently, I poured some more port into my glass and waited. Our host cleared his throat, took his monocle out of his eye and in a quiet voice, trembling slightly with emotion, said: 'Now then, you young fellahs. I want to tell you as an old man who's knocked around a bit in me time, that in my opinion, none of you will ever again be privileged to set eyes on a prettier face than that of our young friend here tonight. I refer, of course, to old Harry Mainwaring's girl. Look after her, you chaps, and if you're lucky enough to get a dance with her tonight treat her like a piece of priceless porcelain . . . by God, that girl's a good-looker!' And our host sat down heavily, perspiring somewhat.

I came to know Zara in time and by God she *was* a good-looker and as sweet as they come. She married first Ronnie Strutt, who later became Lord Belper, and then in 1949 Peter Cazalet.

During this time I visited many of the great country houses of England. These included Belvoir Castle, Haddon Hall, Hinchingbrooke Hall, Chatsworth, Castle Howard, Leeds Castle, Chirk Castle, Sutton Place, Hill Hall, Himley Hall, Arley Hall, Luton Hoo, Gosford House, Plas Newydd and my stepfather's ancestral home, Lyme Hall in Cheshire.

Arriving for the weekend at one of these large country houses used to be quite an ordeal for a young man. The sheer size of the entrance hall, the endless stone steps and the long corridors were quite alarming, as you followed the footman with your luggage to your bedroom in the West Wing, to be told that dinner was at eight-thirty and that the house-party would assemble in the Great Hall at twenty past.

Few people could unpack one's rather worn and shabby clothing and lay it out on the bed – evening socks so placed to show the holes in them – more pointedly than a butler or footman in a grand house. The whole business of being unpacked for by servants was always a risk. A chap I knew once found that a packet of French letters he'd slipped hopefully into his weekend suitcase had been unpacked by an under-housemaid and placed with his toothbrush in a tumbler on the bathroom shelf. And Brian Johnston once told me about a friend of his who had his cricket bag unpacked by the nanny at a country house where he was staying for a match. When he went up to dress for dinner he found she'd put his protective box on the dressing-table with his shirt studs in it.

Large country houses always had and still have a certain odd smell of hotplate, silver polish and methylated spirits. I think it comes from the butler's pantry but wafts through the swing doors from the servants' quarters to mingle with the delicious, expensive scent of the lady guests.

The 9th Duke of Rutland, father of the present Duke, was a great stickler for old customs and when I first used to stay at Belvoir in the 'thirties as a friend of his daughters, Ursula and Isobel Manners, it was necessary to bring for the weekend a white tie, tails and white waistcoat for wearing at dinner. Any number of Isobel's and Ursula's young men, whom they'd collected in London or in the hunting field, and to whom they'd said 'Come for the weekend,' used to arrive at Belvoir, not unnaturally, with only a short coat (dinner jacket) and a black tie. Accustomed to this constantly recurring disaster for the unwitting male guest, the butler at Belvoir always kept a big cupboard filled with tail coats, white waistcoats and white ties of all sizes — like Moss Bros — for loaning to the embarrassed young weekender. I often wonder whether the 9th Duke ever realized that a number of the men's coats round his glittering dinner table came from his own butler's private supply. Staying in one wing of Belvoir Castle today with Charles, the present Duke, his decorative wife Frances and their children, is delightfully cosy and informal, as befits the 1970s.

The only time I ever stayed at Chatsworth ended, alas, in tears. The occasion was a young men's shoot in 1937, organized for the Devonshire heir, Billy Burlington, as he then was, and his younger brother, Andrew, the present incumbent. Chatsworth was still inhabited at that time by the old Duke and Duchess, who were our hosts.

The guns were, as far as I can recall, Billy, Andrew, Hugh

Fraser, James MacDonnell, Derek Parker-Bowles, David Ormsby-Gore (later Lord Harlech) and a few others; the girls *inter alios* were Anne Bowes-Lyon, Fiona Colqhoun, two pretty Grosvenor girls, Irene Haig and Arbell MacIntosh, who was a Devonshire grand-daughter. I can't remember who the other guests were. I do recall that the old Duke of Devonshire shot his pheasants from the hip off his shooting-stick, so that when at one drive, I was next to him in the line, my loader advised me, as soon as His Grace started blasting away, to lie down flat and keep still. This seemed to me a pity, as the pheasants were flying well, but I've since heard that this advice was well taken.

When lunch was served in a farm building, Billy and Andrew suggested that I should sit next to the old man, on the grounds that he'd known my grandfather when he, the Duke, had been Governor-General of Canada. No one else seemed keen to oblige. So I did my duty and had an interesting lunch, although the Duke's soft-boiled egg dribbled down his chin a good deal as he talked about the CPR.

The trouble began after dinner on the Saturday night. The champagne and port had flowed freely and Andrew Cavendish was in a rowdy mood. Wild games were played, the girls were chased all over the house and faintly obscene things were painted with lipstick on some of the marble statues. As was so often the way in the great houses of England, a few billiard cues got broken and a certain amount of glass as well. Nobody saw the Duchess to say goodnight, and we all eventually staggered off to bed. But the next morning, when the footman came in to call me with early morning tea, he informed me that cars would be leaving for the station at nine-thirty and that Her Grace expected the young guests to be ready at that hour to leave for London. We were being thrown out.

I travelled down to London in a railway compartment with Billy and Anne Bowes-Lyon. We were all three a trifle annoyed by the events of the previous night for which we rather blamed Andrew. We felt ourselves innocent of the worst excesses and victims of circumstance. Billy Burlington was the nicest and best-looking young man you could find anywhere. He later married Kathleen ('Kick') Kennedy, the charming sister of President J.F.K., only to be killed in action soon after, while serving with the Coldstream Guards in Belgium in 1944. Kick was tragically killed in an air accident soon after the war. Thus in the fullness of time Andrew succeeded to the Dukedom and became a thoroughly responsible, gentle, popular and kind-hearted Lord of Chatsworth.

Mention of Kick Kennedy reminds me of one of the quainter experiences awaiting a young man at a weekend house-party in the 'thirties, if he happened to be, as I am, a Roman Catholic. Almost without fail, shortly before the guests retired to bed on the Saturday night, the hostess would say: 'Church in the morning at eleven.' The young guests would nod their heads politely. I then had to take a pace forward and say boldly: 'But Lady Fotheringay, I'm afraid I'm a Roman Catholic.' 'Oh, I see,' would come the faintly shocked reply.

It was thus my lot to go separately to Mass in my own car, if I had it with me, or in one of the family cars (most inconvenient) if I hadn't. I used to pray for another RC in the party so that I would not be alone in creating this inconvenience. Often there was a Catholic servant in the house. So it was: 'Our cook is a Catholic, if you don't mind going with her. We always send her in.' Or there was an Irish housemaid or a visiting French lady's maid. Sometimes it was a fellow guest or guests, plus a servant or two. I remember volunteering at a weekend with Lord and Lady Kemsley at Farnham to drive Kick Kennedy into Mass in Windsor, while the others sat by the fire and read the Sunday papers. For some reason I could not find the Catholic Church, where I had worshipped for years while at Eton; it was in a back street and we drove round and round Windsor in circles, becoming hysterical. We were late anyway, as Mass was at 10.30 and we'd left Farnham at twenty-five past. So, after a brief consultation and probing of each other's consciences, Kick and I decided to call it a day, bought some sweets and a *News of the World* and headed back for the Berry home, where we felt honour bound to confess to the house-party that we hadn't been able to confess to God after all.

One weekend staying at Plas Newydd with the Angleseys, I had the considerable thrill of being driven to Mass in Bangor with Mr and Mrs Evelyn Waugh; unfortunately the great author hardly spoke at all on the way and seemed to be getting himself into a state of grace, taking it all very seriously, as converts often do.

Plas Newydd was the happiest 'big house' I have known, because of the adorable Paget family, whose home it was and still is. Life in the summer at P.N. was a dream sequence of lovely

Paget girls, laughter and music and swimming and tennis and the sloping green lawns overlooking the Menai Straits across to neighbouring Vaynol, where Michael Duff held court. And all the while Rex Whistler painted away at his now famous family mural in the dining-room, his labour of love for the Anglesey tribe, portraying himself as a small figure in gardener's clothes sweeping leaves with a broom.

It was from Plas Newydd in the summer of 1938 just before the Munich Crisis that we all saw Duff and Diana Cooper and their gorgeous niece, Liz Paget, off aboard the Admiralty yacht *Enchantress* for a cruise in the Adriatic. Duff Cooper was the Paget girls' very special uncle, always witty and youthful and full of fun despite the cares of state. Plas Newydd was a lovely house to stay in and Charlie and Marjorie Anglesey must rank as the most beautiful, glamorous couple who ever graced the English scene.

Chirk Castle in the 'thirties offered something of the same atmosphere to a young man. Margot Howard de Walden had only one son but masses of daughters and there too the house rang with the laughter of happy girls. But life was quite hardy at Chirk. There was a schoolroom window some fifteen feet above a lawn from which a young guest had to leap to prove his manhood. Sometimes, on a warm night, the Scott-Ellis girls and their young guests would sleep out on the lawn in a long line of fleabags, to be called in the morning by a liveried footman stepping carefully among the snoring bodies.

A visit to Luton Hoo was always amusing in the earlier days, when old Lady Ludlow, Sir Harold Wernher's mother, was the occupant. She was a remarkable old lady with a facial twitch and a grating voice that sounded like East End cockney. I remember one summer day at Luton Hoo in 1933, when we all came bounding into the great dining-room from the tennis courts for tea. The most enormous spread had been laid out on the table. There were crab and lobster sandwiches, cream buns, éclairs, mountains of strawberries and ice cream, jugs of orangeade and much, much more. Three liveried footmen stood by.

As we all trooped in goggle-eyed in our white flannels and blazers, old Lady Ludlow hobbled in behind us leaning on her stick and twitching. 'Come along, boys and gels,' she croaked, ' 'elp yerselves, it's all free, yer know! Nothing to pay.'

The same evening, when champagne cocktails were served before dinner, every guest took with his glass from the silver tray a small embroidered napkin with which to wipe his fingers or the stem of his glass. Lady Ludlow came up to me and one of the girls I was talking to and with a wicked wink muttered out of the side of her mouth, 'Don't you pinch those things; most of my guests do, use 'em as pocket 'ankies'; then she drifted away to join another group. She was a panic. I stayed at Luton years later, after the war, when Harold and Zia Wernher were in residence, and had the opportunity of seeing the fabulous collection of ornaments and objets d'art in the museum there, including the Fabergé snuffboxes and other works of art made for Lady Zia's relations, who were members of the Russian Imperial Family.

Lyme Park in Cheshire, the Legh family home for over six centuries, was unfortunately given away in 1940 by my step-father's brother, the second Lord Newton, to the National Trust who leased it to the Stockport Corporation. We had stayed there nearly every Christmas as children, played hide-and-seek and sar-dines all over the great Elizabethan house and cycled about in the park; later my brother and I learned to shoot pheasants there. It was sad and eerie to visit the place a few years ago as a tripper, pay-ing at the gate, and going over the house with a guide. Every corner held a memory of childhood and the old nursery and schoolroom wing where we wore away the carpets over the years, had become dormitories for visiting seminars of Lancashire students or Nation-al Coal Board courses in management or delegate conferences of the National Union of Mineworkers. Some of the pictures and a lot of the furniture were still there on display in the reception rooms, the Long Gallery and the Great Hall. But the feeling of a home had gone out of the house, like the breath and living spirit goes out of a man when he dies.

Another fine house, no longer a family residence, was Leeds Castle, near Maidstone. Lady Baillie, who lived there, spent a for-tune having it done up luxuriously in medieval style. Stone steps were left uncovered and some new ones were installed, worn away by machines, and red rope banisters were attached to the walls. It was the acme of opulence and comfort and the weekends I spent there before and after the Second World War were some of the most interesting and colourful in my experience. Olive Baillie was a daughter of Lord Queenborough, thus a sister of Dorothy Paget of racing fame; she was also a Whitney on her mother's side and after a former marriage to Charlie Winn had foundered, she had married Sir Adrian Baillie, a charming, gentle baronet, who was the Member of Parliament for Tonbridge and happened to be fascinated by films. So it was that the prevailing atmosphere at Leeds Castle hovered somewhere between the movie business and politics.

Ministers of the Crown and movie stars mingled under Olive's roof over the years. Her two oldest and most faithful friends, who remained close to her after Adrian died, were Lord Margesson, once the Conservative Party Chief Whip, and Geoffrey Lloyd, once Minister of Fuel. I was first invited to Leeds before the war as a young man about town, who happened to know and dance with Pauline Winn, Olive's elder daughter by her first marriage, and one incident I recall at that time illustrates the gulf that can exist between what might be called public life and show business. The famous and formidable Lady Willingdon was staying and I had been next to her at Sunday lunch. After lunch I walked out with her on to the croquet lawn, for it was a warm sunny day. Also at lunch – I think he'd motored down for the day – was Ray Milland, who at the time was just about the biggest star in Hollywood with Robert Taylor, Clark Gable and Gary Cooper.

As I strolled with Lady Willingdon, widow of the former Governor-General of Canada and Viceroy of India, she spotted Ray Milland across the croquet lawn smoking a cigar. 'Who is that young man?' she asked me. I said to her: 'That's Ray Milland, the film star.' She looked blank. 'Introduce me,' she commanded. I left her and went up, a touch uneasy, to Ray Milland, whom I hadn't yet met – so vast was the lunch party. 'Excuse me,' I said, 'Lady Willingdon wants to meet you.' 'Lady who?' 'Lady Willingdon, standing just over there,' I said. 'Who's she?' asked Milland. But I couldn't enlighten him any further, for Lady W. had come up meanwhile and was saying to Mr Milland, 'Escort me round the lawn, young man; they tell me you're an actor on the films.' It was a fascinating piece of chemistry. I cannot imagine what they talked about.

An early memory of some theatrical interest is a visit in my teens to Himley Hall in Worcestershire, the home of Lord and Lady Ednam, as they then were. He later lost his lovely wife, Rosie, in an air crash, and eventually became Lord Dudley. As a school friend of young Billy Ward, the son and heir, I remember going down from the schoolroom to the drawing-room after tea to play charades and other parlour games with the grown-up members of the house-party, which was a large one.

An elderly lady called Madame Boucicault amused us all by sticking a handkerchief on top of her head and hobbling across the room with a stick and puffed-out cheeks. It was her celebrated imitation of Queen Victoria and I later discovered that she was the famous actress, Irene Vanburgh. Also staying at Himley on that occasion was Lord Ednam's stepmother, Gertrude, Countess of Dudley, who as many readers will know, was Gertie Millar, the musical comedy star of Edwardian times. She joined in happily for the charades with the young guests, while Madame Boucicault retired upstairs to rest. It was an interesting close-up of two very celebrated ladies from opposite ends of the stage: the petite, round-faced, sparkling little 'pekinese' Gertie Millar, still pretty as paint in her seventies; and the grey, elegant, aristocratic-looking Irene Vanburgh, a queen of the straight theatre.

Looking back on the great country houses I've stayed in or visited, I suppose that what gives them their special atmosphere and aura of importance is that in so many of them great political ideas have been exchanged, decisions of state made and public careers embarked upon. If you read all the political biographies and autobiographies of recent British history, the lives of Curzon, Crewe, Lansdowne, Lloyd George, Bonar Law, Asquith, Halifax, Duff Cooper, not to mention the lighter reminiscences of people at the centre of power in their time, the Diana Coopers, Harold Nicolsons, Beaverbrooks, and much of the Edwardian 'gossip' literature involving such personalities as Jenny Churchill, Daisy Warwick, Alice Keppel and others, you will be transported from one famous country house to another. You will read of house parties, balls and political gatherings at Blenheim, Belvoir, Ditchley, Chatsworth, Sutton, Knole, Trent, Mereworth, Leeds, Eaton, Knowsley, Gosford . . . the list is endless. Alas, many of those noble edifices are no longer peopled by armies of butlers, footmen, housemaids and smart guests. Some have become schools, technical colleges, asylums, museums or just wrecks. Some are holding grimly on. To misquote Noël Coward: 'The stately homes of England, how dismally they stand, to prove the nobs no longer possess the upper hand. . . .'

— FIVE —

Grace and Favour

Loelia, Duchess of Westminster, who as Loelia Ponsonby grew up
in St James's Palace, once wrote a book called *Grace and Favour*
which said more or less all there is to be said about living in a royal
palace. So I will be brief.

The section of St James's Palace occupied by her father, Lord
Sysonby, who was Keeper of the Privy Purse to King George V,
was the corner block to the left of the clock tower as you face it
from St James's Street, going round into Marlborough Gate. The
front door, with a small brass plate bearing the occupant's name,
faces across to Hardy's fishing shop in Pall Mall; the inner side
looks out over the Colour Court.

This very same house was allotted to Joey by King Edward
VIII on his accession to the throne in January 1936 and thus
became our home for nineteen years.

It was in the large room off the drawing-room with windows
overlooking Marlborough Gate and the Colour Court that the
Duke of Cumberland is said to have murdered his valet in 1810;
and there my brother and I slept, Tommy until he went off in 1937
to Canada; I until I married in 1948 and moved into a flat in
Chesham Street.

My early years as a resident at St James's were what might be
called my 'wild oats' years. I was twenty when we moved in and
was at that time leading a very social, extravagantly gay life, endlessly dining out, going to cocktail parties, dances and nightclubs.

Thus on many a warm summer night I would stagger out of the
Cabaret Club or The Bag of Nails or The Nest, up to the eyeballs
in gin, fall into a taxi and croak to the cabby: 'St James's Palace,
please.' To which the cabby would reply with heavy sarcasm:

42

'Sure you don't mean Buckingham Palace, cock? Now then, what's it to be, mate, your proper address or Bow Street. I'm easy.'

Once, when I said sheepishly to a taxi-driver: 'No really. I do live there. I really do,' the reply came from the front seat: 'Yes and I live at No. 10 Downing Street, sonny. Come on, stop messing abaht. Where do you want to go?'

Well, dash it, one was a bit the worse for wear and, often as not the old bow-tie was somewhat askew and there was just a dash of lipstick on the old stiff shirtfront. Can you blame those cabbies?

A minor hazard in the small hours was trying to reach the front door, insert the key and dive in unobserved during the few seconds that the sentry from the box under the clock tower elected to march to the corner of Marlborough Gate and back again. If he happened to reach our front door just as I was struggling desperately to get my key in the lock, he seemed to crash his boots down with extra force on the pavement, as he turned about, the sound echoing all the way up St James's Street. I used to think with a sense of guilt that this was an ordinary guardsman's way of expressing his disapproval of a system that allowed 'grace and favour' residences to be occupied by drunken young men in dinner jackets fumbling with latchkeys at four o'clock in the morning.

When the Abdication crisis broke, I was living at St James's and still working at Nathan & Rosselli's in the City. Since Joey had been equerry and close personal friend to the Prince of Wales for fifteen years, had accompanied him on his tours to Australia, Japan, Canada and India and was still at his side when he acceded to the throne in 1936, it stands to reason that Wallis Simpson had been a constant topic of conversation at our house in Norfolk Square from about 1934 onwards. My brother and I had been boys at Eton in 1933, when one Sunday morning in early summer we were driven over from school dressed in our Eton tails and top-hats to lunch at Fort Belvedere, where mother and Joey were weekend guests of the Prince of Wales.

It was a memorable day for not only were Prince George, later the Duke of Kent, his equerry, Humphrey Butler, his wife 'Poots' and Lady Dalkeith present but also a Mr and Mrs Ernest Simpson. The three outstanding memories I have of that Sunday afternoon are tearing across Virginia Water in a tiny outboard motor-boat piloted by Prince George; being driven back to Eton by Prince George down the Long Walk at great speed in a gorgeous black

Bentley with red lines on it and his Alsatian, Duska, in the back; and asking my mother, in her bedroom after tea, about the very talkative American woman, who teased the Prince of Wales during lunch – which he seemed to enjoy – and why her husband said so little during the day. My mother's reply was that she was 'just someone the Prince met in America' and the subject was promptly changed.

Over the next three years I was to learn more of Mrs Simpson and eventually sat next to her at dinner one night in October 1936 at the house of mutual friends, the John Dodges. After dinner, as I strummed some tunes on the piano, she asked me to play 'Over the Sea to Skye', a piece which had been featured by the pipers at King George V's funeral earlier that year. She plainly had a romantic vision of the new King as the 'King over the Water', Virginia Water, I supposed; or was it because he so often wore a kilt? Soon after that dinner at the Dodges' the Bishop of Bradford delivered his now famous speech to a diocesan conference. The next evening Mother and Joey attended the equally famous dinner-party round the corner at Stornaway House at which Lord Beaverbrook told a number of his friends close to the throne that the British press could hold back no longer and were going to break the story; and with key people like Sir Ulick Alexander, Sir Alan Lascelles, Sir Walter Monkton and others popping in and out of our house with the latest news, I knew with certainty that King Edward was about to give up his throne. Like most people, I was sad, because he was a magnetic, glamorous figure with dynamism and all the charm in the world; but any fool could see that 'she' could never be accepted as Queen by the British public. And there was no compromise.

It fell to Joey to embark on HMS *Fury* at 0130 hrs that foggy December morning, which happened to be his birthday, and sail with ex-King Edward VIII into exile. Not long ago I made contact with the officer who had commanded *Fury* on that historic voyage, to discover what he could remember of it.

Captain Cecil Howe received me most courteously in his small flat on the front at Lee-on-Solent, overlooking the Isle of Wight, and, prompted by his wife, described his most unusual and memorable assignment as a destroyer captain.

It seems he received his highly secret sailing orders at the very last minute and was obliged to borrow from the Royal Yacht some

1 The author (seated) with his mother, Betty and Tom. 1919.

2 The author's grandfather, the first Lord Shaughnessy. 1916.

3 A ride in Joey's Rover motor car. 1923.

4 The author's father (right), killed in the trenches aged 28.

5   Piers 'Joey' Legh and The Prince of Wales. 1932.

6 Lyme Park, the Legh family seat in Cheshire.

7 The author (left) showing the Australian cricketers Woodfull and Oldfield around Eton.

SPECIAL EDITION

JUDGE FOR YOURSELF—
It's the whisky
BLACK & WHITE

Evening Standard

The Premier Havana Cigar
BOLIVAR
CORONAS

No. 35,038   LONDON, SATURDAY, DECEMBER 12, 1936   ONE PENNY

PRINCE EDWARD SAILS

1.45 a.m. Departure from Portsmouth in Destroyer

King George VI. to Be Proclaimed To-day

CEREMONY BROADCAST TO THE EMPIRE

Accession Council Meet: M.P.s Take Oath This Afternoon

THE DESTROYER FURY

Proclamation of King George VI.

PRINCE EDWARD SAILED AWAY FROM ENGLAND TO-DAY AT 1.45 A.M. A FEW HOURS AFTER THE EMPIRE AND THE WORLD HAD HEARD HIS BROADCAST WORDS OF FAREWELL.

He left Fort Belvedere just before 11 p.m., having taken leave of the new King, Queen Mary, the Princess Royal, the Duke of Gloucester and the Duke of Kent.

Prince Edward drove to Portsmouth.

About midnight two cars and two shooting brakes passed through the Unicorn Gate of the dockyard there.

Prince Edward arrived at Portsmouth some time later in another car. The car pulled up near the Guildhall in the centre of the city.

The last civilian to whom Prince Edward spoke on English soil was Mr. Hale, a signwriter of Portsmouth, whose car had stopped near the Royal car.

The chauffeur of the Royal car asked Mr. Hale the way to the Unicorn Gate. Mr. Hale offered to guide the car, but the chauffeur declined and asked for directions. Mr. Hale gave them.

Prince Edward called from the car, "Thank you very much."

Commander-in-Chief's Farewell

The car drove on, but instead of entering the dockyard by the Unicorn Gate it went to the main gate.

A sergeant of the dockyard police walked across and challenged it. Prince Edward leaned forward and spoke to him. The sergeant sprang to attention and saluted. The car passed into the dockyard.

At the Unicorn Gate Admiral Sir William Fisher, Commander-in-Chief, Portsmouth, was waiting.

When Sir William heard that Prince Edward had arrived he drove across to the waterside to greet him. They shook hands.

Soon afterwards Prince Edward went aboard the destroyer Fury. The Fury, which is commanded by Commander C. L. Howe, put to sea unescorted.

Later in the morning Reuter reported the harbour authorities at Havre had been warned of the possibility of the Fury arriving there.

Reports published to-day that Prince Edward would leave in the Admiralty yacht Enchantress were incorrect. This morning the Enchantress was still in the Tidal Basin at Portsmouth.

THE Accession Council are meeting this morning at St. James's Palace to draw up the Proclamation announcing the accession to the Throne of King George VI.

This afternoon the Proclamation is being read first at St. James's Palace and then at Charing Cross, Temple Bar and on the steps of the Royal Exchange.

The ceremony at St. James's Palace will be broadcast to the Empire and to many foreign lands.

The House of Commons are meeting this afternoon so that members may take the Oath of Allegiance to the new King George. The process will be continued on Monday.

George VI. was proclaimed at Pretoria to-day. A salute of 21 guns was fired.

Mrs. Simpson's Servants

THREE maids, a cook and a chauffeur belonging to the household staff of Mrs. Simpson arrived at 2 a.m. to-day at Dieppe in the cross-Channel steamer from Newhaven. They left Dieppe by car (says Reuter).

Details of Proclamation ceremonies—PAGE FIVE.

The HON. PIERS LEGH, who is with Prince Edward.

8   The *Evening Standard* on Abdication Day.

bed linen, crockery, glasses and other necessities for the trip, as well as an experienced steward who knew the ex-King and would serve him during the crossing. An element of 'Keystone Cops' comedy crept into the tragic departure of King Edward VIII from his kingdom when in the small hours of 12 December the royal car entered Portsmouth Dockyard by the wrong gate, leaving the C-in-C Portsmouth and his party waiting in vain at the correct gate. Hearing that the ex-King had somehow arrived at *Fury's* berth, the C-in-C had to jump into his car and tear round to the quayside, arriving just in time for the simple departure ceremony. At 0130 hrs ex-King Edward eventually embarked with Joey, Ulick Alexander and two detectives, Chief Inspector Storrier and Detective Sergeant Atfield. There also embarked the Surgeon-Commander from the Royal Yacht, whom Joey had insisted should travel with them, in case the ex-King's state of mental stress should cause him to require any medical attention while at sea.

Missing from the party was the ex-King's valet, Crisp, who had declined to accompany his royal master into exile. Thus the Duke of Windsor (as he was henceforth to be known) had to carry his small Cairn bitch up the gangway himself. The Cairn, Cora, later made a mess in Commander Howe's quarters, but that is another story. Worried that there was nobody aboard to valet the Duke during the voyage or indeed to look after his clothes in exile, Joey approached the steward from the Royal Yacht. He was willing to accept the role but had only his uniform with him. Commander Howe had a civilian suit in his quarters and offered to lend it to the steward if it would fit him. It would. The immediate problem was solved and HRH would have a valet after all, at least until a permanent manservant could be found and sent out to him.

As soon as the royal exile was embarked Howe weighed anchor and HMS *Fury* slid silently out of Portsmouth, but only as far as a point one mile or so off Bembridge in the Isle of Wight, where she was to lie off for some hours so the Duke could get some sleep. But the exiled King was not surprisingly in a state of high nervous tension and restlessness that night. He sat up in the wardroom until four in the morning, drinking brandy and going over the events of the last few weeks. Joey and Ulick Alexander, already exhausted by the strain of the whole abdication trauma and very short of sleep, longed for HRH to retire to his cabin so they themselves could turn in.

Captain Howe told me that around three-thirty in the morning Joey, drooping with fatigue, came up to find him in his quarters and begged him to come down to the wardroom and relieve him and Ulick by engaging the Duke in conversation. Howe most nobly obliged, so the two exhausted courtiers were able to tumble into their bunks. Shortly after four the Duke succumbed finally to the arms of Morpheus.

With the exiled King fast asleep, Howe sailed quietly out of the Solent into the Channel and reached Boulogne at 1540 the following afternoon to tie up at a berth which had been completely sealed off from public view and was heavily policed by the French Garde Mobile. Here the Duke exercised Cora on her lead along the quay, received on board various French officials and bade farewell to Ulick Alexander, who took leave of his boss and caught the next boat back to Folkestone.

It was not until 1950 hrs that evening that the Duke, Joey and the two detectives finally disembarked from *Fury,* thanking Commander Howe and his company for a comfortable and agreeable voyage, and climbed into the special Pullman car drawn up on the quay for the rail journey on to Paris and Austria.

The steward from the Royal Yacht, however, dressed in his borrowed suit, did not after all enter the train as valet to the royal exile. The French authorities, notwithstanding the unusual circumstances, refused to allow the man ashore since he carried no passport.

Thus the ex-King of England went into exile with no one to press his trousers until he reached Schloss Enzesfeld.

Joey told us later that those early days and nights at Baron Eugene de Rothschild's Schloss were pretty dreadful. The ex-King was predictably depressed and frustrated. He was separated from Wallis and he'd given up his Crown. So he consoled himself in the evenings by playing the jazz-drums very loud and long to a gramophone record; he also drank quite a lot of brandy, and performed his celebrated imitation of Winston Churchill trying to persuade him not to abdicate: 'Sir, we must fight. . . .'

As the stepson of a courtier at the centre of the crisis, I sensed the historical gravity of the Abdication. But as a young stockbroker's clerk, I could not help reflecting how much money I could have made with my advance knowledge of the press breaks by becoming a 'bear' and selling gilt edged short, picking it up in the same account, once official news of the King's possible departure had knocked the City for six.

But I resisted the temptation and in due course Joey returned from Austria in answer to a royal summons to Sandringham, where King George VI and his Queen asked him to join their Household and stay on at his 'grace and favour' house in St James's Palace. Seeing that his duty was to the Throne rather than to the man, Joey agreed. And the Duke of Windsor never forgave him.

They met on and off over the years that followed, mostly at Lord Dudley's house in Hertfordshire, where the Duke used to stay on his visits here, usually without the Duchess. But the warmth had gone out of their relationship. Joey found him just a little cool. The reasons were obvious to all of us. Joey was an exceptionally conventional man, steeped in court etiquette, protocol and What Was Done. Although he was himself married to an American, and had lived discreetly for years with the knowledge of the Prince of Wales' deep fondness for Mrs Freda Dudley Ward, whom he liked and admired, he disapproved from the start of the Prince's liaison with Wallis Simpson and showed it. While others round the King such as Lord Brownlow, a cousin of Joey's by marriage, Lady Colefax and Lady Cunard's set more or less encouraged the affair by inviting Wallis to parties for the King, Joey never did. Wallis knew he disapproved and consequently she disapproved of Joey. This rubbed off on the King and the outcome was always predictable.

When Joey died in 1955 and my mother died the next day, the Windsors were kind enough to send a very large wreath with a formal message of condolence to us all. But an age-old comradeship between two men that had begun during the First World War had been broken by the infatuation of one of them with a woman. A familiar story.

— SIX —

A West End Theatrical Manager at Twenty

In the months between the departure of King Edward VIII and the coronation of King George VI, I continued stockbroking by day and dancing by night.

As Joey was now with the new King and Queen, my social status remained unimpaired. During this period I was even invited to one of Lady Cunard's famous luncheon parties at 7 Grosvenor Square and to her box at the opera.

But moving in such high social circles was by no means the ultimate aim of my life. I was by now hopelessly and irrevocably stage-struck and in love with everything to do with the theatre, films, music and dancing. But how could a junior stockbroker's clerk fulfil such theatrical ambitions? I little realized in the early spring of 1937 that within three months I would be a West End theatrical manager. Let me dwell for a moment on my dreams of a life in the theatre. It had all begun at the age of nine when I was taken to the Palace Theatre, London to see *No, No, Nanette* with Binnie Hale, Joseph Coyne, George Grossmith and others. I already had a fairly good ear for melody and harmony and, on this occasion, I can distinctly remember coming home afterwards in a taxi and making straight for the Bluthner Grand in our drawing-room at 43 Norfolk Square, opening the keyboard lid – not the main lid, which would have meant removing shawls, vases and family photographs – and picking out 'Tea for Two' and 'I Want to Be Happy' with one finger in the key of C major.

From that day on I was taken to countless other musical comedies, revues and thrillers. Every school holidays or long leave meant 'a theatre' and, although my brother and I got through masses of thrillers – mostly by Edgar Wallace – and farces by Ben

48

Travers, we rarely missed a new musical. I think my mother felt musical shows were safe: colourful scenery and dresses, simple, wholesome jokes, cheerful tunes. We saw *Hit The Deck, Rose Marie, The Desert Song,* the Astaires in *Funny Face,* all the Bobby Howes-Binnie Hale shows, the Stanley Lupino and Laddie Cliff shows, progressing later to the more sophisticated revues, such as Coward's *Words and Music,* Cole Porter's *Wake Up and Dream; Bitter Sweet, Cavalcade, Show Boat,* the list is endless. In the late 'thirties as I became older and more sophisticated in taste I developed a craze for Rodgers and Hart. *On Your Toes* remains my favourite example of their brilliant work together. I went to countless shows through and after the war, caring mainly for the score, ears alert for tunes, tunes, tunes. And clever, singable lyrics.

The 'book' of a 'book' show has never worried me all that much. It can be about anything, as long as the musical numbers are there. I couldn't begin to relate the plots of any of the shows I've seen over fifty years of playgoing but I can still play, hum and possibly sing the words of all sorts of obscure, forgotten numbers by da Silva, Brown and Henderson, Joseph Tunbridge, Johnny Green or Vivian Ellis from ages back. I do not claim to match the extraordinary expertise of people like Frank Muir and Denis Norden, whose minds appear to be veritable archives of jokes and music. But I am pretty good at playing at least a few bars of anything I've ever heard and registered by ear.

I regard the pure musical comedy as an art form as much as opera and operetta. There are rules and traditions to be observed and it has always interested me how, in the United States where this genre of entertainment really began, musical comedy has always been taken very seriously, respected and skilfully done.

Perhaps these shows depended on their stars and would today die without them, however much audiences enjoyed the quaint, old fashioned text, jokes and lyrics. With modern staging costs it's a gamble anyway; it's far too expensive now to experiment with large-scale musical productions.

After fifty years as a musical comedy fan, I would – if interviewed on the radio – be asked no doubt to recall some of the highspots I can remember. I would start with something that anybody who ever saw it must still remember: the drunk scene between Leslie Henson and Sydney Howard in the Gershwin show *Funny Face.* The Astaires were quite dreamy in it and I fell in love with

Adele. But how that drunk scene sticks. Then there was the male chorus in *The Three Musketeers* at Drury Lane singing a blood-stirring march, 'We Are the Musketeers' by Rudolph Friml. It was the natural successor to Sigmund Romberg's 'Riff Song' in *The Desert Song*. The duel and death of Karl Linden at the First Act curtain of *Bitter Sweet* is immortal, the curtain falling in a silence broken only by the sobbing of Ivy St Helier as La Crevette. Binnie Hale singing 'Spread a Little Happiness' in *Mr Cinders* at the Hippodrome.

Then there is the choreography of Cole Porter's number 'You and the Night and the Music' in the American revue *Stop Press*; Maisie Gay waiting for a bus in Coward's *This Year of Grace* at the London Pavilion. Jack Buchanan and Elsie Randolph doing 'Fancy Our Meeting' in *That's a Good Girl*; and that will have to do.

I sometimes regret the gradual passing of the old musical comedy traditions. I always loved the way that, after a big number was over and the chorus had danced off to applause, one or two of the principals would come straight on to advance the plot with the most banal dialogue like: 'I say Percy have you seen Myrtle this morning?' 'Yes. She went down to the beach with that cad Summers.' 'Ah, I thought they seemed a bit lovey dovey at the Yacht Club party last night.' 'Lovey dovey?' 'Yes, you know, lovey dovey. Summers is awfully keen on Myrtle.' 'Lovey dovey. I thought Myrtle was keen on Summers. You know, the other way round.' 'Oh, you mean dovey lovey. . . .' Laughter.

I also adore the quiet, soulful reprise of the main love tune, sometimes in the minor key after the inevitable misunderstanding and parting of the lovers, the climax to the first half. They have quarrelled and he is left alone, she having flounced off with her aunt. He sits there all sad and deserted, fingering the pair of gloves she's left behind, while the orchestra reprises their hit number softly on muted strings. It was so often Bobby Howes and what pathos he achieved. This 'reprise' technique is how tunes are sold and it is a great tradition. Puccini used it, always, and he was the greatest of them all.

Moving today through modern, changed London, past West End theatres, I often get attacks of acute nostalgia, as I glance from my car at, say, the London Pavilion, which is probably showing a film called 'I Was a Nazi Nymphomaniac'. It makes me wonder what the hell Cochran would have thought. Muck like that being projected on to a screen on the stage, where Jessie Matthews and Sonnie Hale sang 'A Room With a View'. Or whether the ghost of Stanley Lupino still haunts the old site of the Shaftesbury Theatre up by the Palace, where so many of his shows were staged. In those days you came out humming the tunes into cheerful, crowded but not jammed streets, filled with English people. And you could always get a taxi.

But let us return to the spring of 1937.

I had more or less grown up with a certain Michael Morris. We'd been nursery mates and fellow Roman Catholics at Eton and I'd continued to bump into him on and off since school days. He'd since become Lord Killanin and a notable Fleet Street journalist with a wide range of friends and acquaintances.

When I collided with him at a cocktail party that spring he told me that Beverley Nichols, whom he knew well (and who incidentally had been, since *Cry Havoc*, rather a hero of mine), had just written and devised a whole revue by himself, sketches, lyrics, music and all in an attempt to out-Noël Mr Coward, whom he admired and envied.

Frances Day, the blonde bombshell of the 'thirties, was to star; John Mills was to be her leading man; the owners of the Saville Theatre in Shaftesbury Avenue were prepared to invest the theatre rent for six weeks as equity; there was some backing from an American friend of Ivor Novello's called Richard Diefendorfer Rose; a producer, C. Denis Freeman, who had recently staged a hit revue at the Saville called *Spread It Abroad* was eager to direct; and they needed only another £8,000 to put the show on. The revue was to be entitled, on account of it being Coronation year, *Floodlight*. Could I help?

Well, I didn't have £8,000. I didn't have £80 but I did have a number of tolerably rich, foolishly adventurous friends, who might be interested in diverting their gambling money from Sandown Park to Shaftesbury Avenue. So I accepted the challenge. The following week I was invited to dine at Beverley's charming house in Ellerdale Road, Swiss Cottage, where I found assembled Frances Day, Denis Freeman, Michael Killanin, Eric Glass, who was Beverley's agent, and Cyril Butcher, who was Beverley's best friend and scheduled for a part in the show.

After dinner Beverley played over the songs he had written for

Floodlight, Frances sang them and in between numbers, Denis read and described the various sketches and ballets. I sat there feeling like Mr Ziegfeld in one of those backstage movies, listening and nodding wisely, while an actor playing Irving Berlin says, 'How's this for a toon, Mr Ziegfeld, it came to me last night in the tub,' and strums the opening phrases of 'Always' or 'What'll I Do?'

Well, Beverley played and Frances sang one of the loveliest waltz melodies I'd ever heard called 'I Will Pray' and Denis explained how this gorgeous number was going to form the exciting and colourful First Act finale, a scene representing the Duchess of Richmond's Ball before Waterloo. I was hooked. Starry-eyed, impressed and awash with Beverley's excellent claret, I resolved to raise the backing if it killed me.

Over the next few days I met a number of affluent friends for lunch in the City and ended up with a small syndicate of backers, among whom were Claud Montagu-Douglas-Scott, an Eton friend and an accomplished pianist; and another Etonian, Lord Ulick Browne, who later married Elma Warren and ran the Nuthouse nightclub throughout the war. It was agreed that I would represent my syndicate's interests and rehearsals for *Floodlight* began in a vast warehouse in the Walworth Road, later moving into the Saville. There ensued an orgy of spending, which even I could soon see was getting out of hand. We had the best of everything and a great deal of self-indulgence was practised by those creatively concerned; but there was regrettably no strong manager, like a Cochran or a Charlot, to control things from the top. Buddy Bradley was hired to stage the tap routines, Freddy Ashton (known in those days only to a small ballet community centred on Sadler's Wells) to choreograph the ballets; Rene Hubert, a monstrously expensive and extravagant Parisian designer, for the costumes and décor; dear little Elsie April, Noël Coward's musical assistant, to arrange, transpose and supplement Beverley's music; Benjamin Frankel to orchestrate and conduct in the pit, and other reputable people in various key positions.

But the lack of strong management and the presence of a number of temperamental young men in the set-up resulted in endless rows, dramas and crises during those stormy rehearsals, most of which I witnessed while cowering out of sight in the back of the stalls. The auditions for 'gentlemen of the chorus' went on for days and proved the deadliest cat-fight of all, as every out-of-work chorus-boy in London minced on and off the stage, while Beverley, Denis and others sat in the stalls disagreeing as to the looks, charm and potential talent of the applicants.

I began to believe the show would never open. One day Frances Day tore an £80 dress into shreds on the stage, because she didn't like it. On another occasion Frances and Hermione Baddeley almost came to blows over their respective billings.

Denis Freeman promised so many of his friends jobs in the revue that we had to keep expanding the male chorus to accommodate them. Frances Day kept on demanding a larger orchestra, Cyril Butcher wanted more lines to speak, the costume and scenic makers wanted their bills settled. As opening time approached the show's budget almost trebled and I had to go to my backers for more money. The 'get-out' figure rose to a totally uneconomic level and things looked very black.

After one chaotic rehearsal Beverley took me off in a taxi to the Garrick Club, where we drowned our anxiety and despair in a champagne cocktail. 'Oh God, Freddy,' he moaned, 'will it ever open?' I murmured without much conviction that I thought it probably would. I'd seen this kind of thing in the movies and it always went big 'on the night' – in the movies.

Beverley remarked that even if the whole thing did collapse in ruins, he would at least 'get a book out of it'. And he did. A year or two later when *Floodlight* was dead and forgotten, Beverley published a novel called *Revue,* which tells in hideous detail of the staging of a West End revue and features all of us, thinly disguised, as 'fictitious' characters bearing no intended resemblance to any living persons.

I appear in the novel as a stupid young playboy called Humbert something. And Frances Day is most cleverly split into two characters, representing the best and the worst of her behaviour: a ghastly, spoilt and temperamental star called Thelma Ganges, and the sweetest, prettiest little understudy, who takes over the lead from Thelma and London by storm, called Fay Pearl.

Floodlight did, in fact, open at the Opera House in Blackpool in July 1937 and I flew up there in a Puss Moth with a pilot friend of Frances Day's to attend the première. After Blackpool a week at the Palace, Manchester and then came the West End first night at the Saville. The show seemed to go reasonably well and we had several curtain calls. Afterwards, to kill time until the early editions came out with reviews of the show, Frances, Rose Paget, Johnny Mills, 'Puffin' Asquith and I repaired to the Florida, where we danced and drank champagne and waited for those dreaded newspapers.

It was generally acknowledged that much of the revue was witty, elegant and charming with many clever sketches and several pretty tunes. However, the whole thing was too precious and lacked the balancing ingredient of robust and virile comedy. This was due to the fact that Beverley had a contract prohibiting the interpolation of anyone else's material. After the Saville opening and the lukewarm-to-hostile London reviews, that clause was urgently rescinded but it was too late. One or two new, broad sketches were brought in, including a very funny slapstick routine devised by Tony Pelissier for Johnny Mills to do as a front-cloth. But the critics had mortally wounded *Floodlight* – rightly in my opinion – and it ran for barely eight expensive weeks at the Saville. Later a provincial tour recouped a little of my syndicate's investment but they still lost heavily. I believe, however, that they had some fun for their money and the project *had* looked good on paper.

As for me, I had the somewhat weird experience of spending the summer of 1937 sitting on my clerk's high stool at Nathan & Rosselli's in Adam's Court just opposite Throgmorton Street, watching the buses go past outside with large posters on their sides proclaiming: 'SAVILLE THEATRE. Evenings at 8.30, Matinees Wed and Sat at 2.30. A. J. Shaughnessy and Richard D. Rose present Frances Day, John Mills and Hermione Baddeley in 'FLOODLIGHT', a new Revue with words and music by Beverley Nichols.' I was a West End impresario and a stockbroker's ledger clerk at the same time. My fellow clerks found it difficult to believe. The head of my department did, however, rumble me and I had to confess that my lengthy absences from the office, when I apparently got lost somewhere between Threadneedle Street and Moorgate, were spent at rehearsals of my revue; so my boss gave me what is sometimes known as a 'bollocking' and in the next breath asked me for a couple of free tickets for his wife and himself.

I cannot think of *Floodlight* without thinking of Frances Day. The show and the star were one and the same experience. On stage Frances had that curious magical charisma known as star quality. Offstage, she was completely fascinating, unpredictable and driven by a sort of crazy originality of mind and boundless physical energy.

During those *Floodlight* days and for some years afterwards I came to know her very well, often escorting her to the Café de Paris for supper after the show, to Ranelagh or Hurlingham to watch the polo, or to her weekend cottage near Esher to swim in her pool of a Sunday. I was only one of a string of bedazzled young men who were under her spell. Apart from anything else, it was fun to be with her, because she was so alive and amusing and outrageous.

One night during the run of *Floodlight* at the Saville, I took Frances back to St James's Palace after supper at Quaglino's to show her where I lived. Needless to say Mama and Joey were away in Scotland for the weekend. Frances, always one for doing something unorthodox, soon spotted that the little window on the top landing opened out on to some leads right over the sentry's head below. Before I could catch her, she had kicked off her shoes, shed her huge white fur wrap and was out on those leads calling down to an astonished young guardsman below: 'Hi, beautiful young man . . . hey, soldier . . . are you happy down there?' Of course the sentry's orders precluded any reply. I remember warning Frances that if she went on too long provoking him to break his silence he might turn round and fire at her, for sentries on duty – I reminded her – always had 'one up the spout'.

I think that last phrase reminded her of the true purpose of her visit, so she climbed in from the leads and we crept into the morning room to help ourselves to a noggin of Joey's whisky.

A day or two before the last Saturday night at the Saville Frances told me that she had chartered a boat in which she planned to take a party of friends, including me, across the Channel to Deauville for the *'grande semaine'*. We were to leave immediately after the last performance. It was, of course, a sort of defiant gesture: 'One show is over, on with the next.' A typical, madcap Frances Day stunt, conceived in a mood of bubbling enthusiasm. The Saturday night soon came, the curtain fell, Benny Frankel and his orchestra for the last time played the house out to reprises of Beverley's most hummable tunes, and we all crowded into Frances' dressing-room, where a great deal of champagne was consumed by the Deauville party and other visitors. At last Frances retired to change, the visitors left and our small group began to load up the cars. We were five, Tony Pelissier, Johnny Mills, Isadore Kerman, who was Frances' solicitor, Greville Howard, younger brother of the gallant Lord Suffolk of bomb-disposal fame, and myself. Frances was also bringing Laura, her dresser – as a chaperone, we joked.

At around midnight we all left by the stage door and piled into two cars, already loaded with crates of champagne and hampers of food. We drove in a convoy down to Portsmouth, arriving at two o'clock in the morning. Some difficulty was experienced in finding the right quay but sooner or later we all stumbled down some slippery steps, humping the champagne and food, fell into a waiting launch and chugged out across the dark harbour to where a large, schooner-like, three-masted sailing ship was riding proudly at anchor.

In the murky darkness the chartered brigantine, *Lady of Avenel,* looked suspiciously like something I'd seen on the movies and, as the launch spluttered to a halt alongside her and a rope ladder was lowered, I fully expected to see pirates peering down at us from the gunwales.

In fact the skipper peered down at us, a stout man in a white sweater and yachting cap, who looked exactly like Charles Laughton, so in my film-sodden, champagne-soaked mind the pirate ship became the *Bounty.* On board were a scratch crew of casual hands, signed on for the trip, which explains what happened later.

Once we were safely over the side and down into the saloon below, another champagne party broke out, which lasted until first light, when we all tumbled, drunk and exhausted, into our bunks.

We were to sail on the morning tide, so when I awoke in my cabin at eleven o'clock on the following Sunday morning to the sound of cranes and seagulls, I was relieved to reflect that the Channel crossing had been accomplished during what had been left of the night before. As I raised my head painfully to look out of the window I heard church bells ringing. The good people of Deauville were being summoned to Mass, I thought. What I saw was the slim grey outline of a British destroyer and a colossal advertisement for Bovril on a hoarding. We were still in Portsmouth Harbour.

It seemed the scratch crew had run into problems with the winch, couldn't get the anchor up and had consequently missed the morning tide. So we had another champagne party and finally

sailed at 3 p.m. The forty-eight hours that followed will remain in
my memory as almost the worst I've ever lived through.

Nausea has ever been my foe. When I was eight I was once taken
by Mama to stay with Admiral and Lady Beatty. One day the
Admiral took me into his study and I stood there, a goggle-eyed
schoolboy, mouth wide open, gazing at all his mementoes: a
tattered flag off a German battleship, bits of shrapnel, his binocul-
ars and the famous cap he wore at Jutland. I was already a bit sea-
struck and that morning spent with the great sailor hero decided
me to join the Navy when I grew up. This ambition was gradually
destroyed over the next few years by heavy seas crossing the
Atlantic and the endless days and nights groaning and reaching
for the basin. In the end I used to feel seasick just going up the
gangway in Southampton.

A pretty fresh headwind was blowing as we left Portsmouth,
and for two days and two nights we pitched and rolled and creaked
and groaned across the storm-tossed Channel. I'm relieved to say
that *all* the men were sick.

Only Frances herself – trust her – remained hale and hearty and
on her feet, skipping about the ship in a blue serge trouser suit and
grey felt hat, shinning up the rigging to take photographs, cooking
stew in the galley and ministering to her pea-green guests, as we lay
in our bunks, praying for an early death.

After what seemed like a week, although it was barely forty-
eight hours, the Normandy coast was sighted and a few hours later
we lowered sail and chugged along on our auxiliary motor to drop
anchor half a mile off Deauville beach.

Nine years later, in the summer of 1944, I was once again
approaching the Normandy coast in a ship but for a very different
purpose; on that occasion the memory of our Deauville trip caused
me to smile a little, until a deafening barrage of gunfire from one of
our battle cruisers lying off Sword Beach wiped the smile off my
face.

As soon as we'd dropped anchor, Frances went below. Minutes
later she reappeared wearing a frilly summer dress, a large picture
hat, gloves and carrying a parasol. We five men, pale and groggy
but somehow attired in tidy suits, dutifully escorted her ashore to
attend the races. There was no time to recover from our nightmare crossing. Frances was on the move again and we had to try
to keep up with her.

As our stomachs gradually settled, we did manage to spend a most happy and hilarious weekend, which included a visit for drinks on board the Mountbattens' yacht and rather a lot of gambling in the casino. But I could not have faced the return trip on board *Lady of Avenel.* Fortunately it was not necessary. I was due to fly on from Deauville to Austria to join a house-party of young people in a chalet rented by Mrs David Margesson for the Salzburg Festival. After three days I said goodbye and my thanks to Frances and left for Vienna, wishing the others a smooth crossing home on that bloody brigantine.

Being involved during the spring and early summer of 1937 with Dickie Rose, the American impresario, it was not surprising that, as Coronation Day approached, Dickie should hint to me that his close friend Ivor Novello would love to see the Coronation procession from our house in St James's Palace. As Mama and Joey were both going to be in the Abbey, Betty, Tom and I were detailed to play host for the day. We were going to entertain a number of friends, as it was, with champagne, sandwiches and a marvellous view from any one of our front side windows or the bathroom leads.

So Ivor came, bringing with him Dorothy Dickson, Eddie Marsh and Dickie Rose. Shortly before the procession came by, Ivor was leaning like an excited child out of Mama's bathroom window, chattering away in a loud, shrill voice, so that all the typists and shopgirls on the pavement down below, who had been there since dawn, had a free show. One or two of them turned round and looked up: 'Coo, look, it's Ivor Novello.' 'It's not, silly.' 'It is, I'd know that face anywhere.' 'Cooee, Ivor . . .' And Ivor waved graciously from Mama's bathroom to his adoring fans below.

Later, when the Coronation coach went by with the new King and Queen inside, sedate and resplendent in their robes, and the bands crashed past playing Elgar's 'Pomp and Circumstance', Ivor became highly emotional, wept a little and gasped: 'Oh, my God, it's too lovely, too moving for words . . . I can't bear it.' Not long afterwards, he wrote a show called *King's Rhapsody* in which there was a coronation.

I had met Ivor once or twice before, the first time when Viola Tree, the mother of my best friend at Eton, David Parsons, had brought him down for the Fourth of June. Since my parents were abroad, I was invited to spend the day in his company with Viola, David, Dennis and Virginia Parsons. Later, around *Floodlight* time, I saw quite a lot of him and came to know him fairly well.

Ivor was very sweet and very, very camp and funny and, as everyone knows, exceptionally kind to elderly actresses and theatre people down on their luck. He personified the romantic musical theatre and the very word 'showmanship'. In most of his Drury Lane epics, he managed to write himself the most marvellous entrances and exits. His subtle line was to present himself as a simple, honest, rather naïve young man, caught up in big, over-blown, extravagant courts or social settings. He exploited 'mod-esty' by playing this retiring young man, creeping on almost apolo-getically when the entire audience knew that he'd devised, written, composed and as the star was carrying the whole colossal pro-duction on his shoulders.

I watched *The Dancing Years* from the wings one night and always remember an incident which really sums up Ivor's impish humour, his colossal self-confidence and his total theatricality. He had just concluded a quiet, moving scene on stage and was making a slow, crestfallen exit to a soft, muted reprise of one of the show's tunes. The audience was transfixed, throats were lumpy, ladies in the dress circle were opening their bags to get their hankies out.

As the lights faded Ivor came quietly off the stage, close to where I was standing. There was a standard lamp in the wings, ready to be taken on and set for a later scene. As Ivor passed the lamp, he snatched the lampshade off it, popped it on his head and said in a loud voice: 'Next year, we're all going to do Aladdin' and with a gay little chorus girl's back kick, disappeared into his dressing room. I cannot imagine how the tear-sodden, stunned audience didn't hear him in the silence.

It was a shock to all, especially the Drury Lane gallery fans, when Ivor ended up in Wormwood Scrubs during the war for some nonsense over a car and petrol coupons. I've never really believed this was the real reason for what Ivor later referred to as 'my in-carceration'. No more than Noël Coward's trouble over currency was, in my opinion, the reason for his continuous and most notice-able omission from the Honours List until it was almost too late. I believe there is still, or was until recently, a deep-rooted prejudice among some elders of the British Establishment, especially the police, against homosexual public figures of the stage.

We all knew of homosexuals in the army, in politics and in the City, but actors could be more easily seen to be gay; and the fact that Ivor spent the war, for which he was anyway too old, basically doing his own thing instead of some official war work, may have attracted the attention of one of those homo-hating police commissioners of the kind that had a famous Shakespearian actor trapped a few years later.

At least Ivor survived prison with his usual sense of humour and came out of it relatively unscathed to resume his brilliant career where it left off. And he died in harness, leaving behind him so many richly haunting melodies, which will be sung and played for ever and ever. One of them, 'Rose of England', would make a superb National Anthem, an honour Ivor would have dearly loved.

—— SEVEN ——

Nights at the Opera

My stay near Salzburg with France Margesson and her two daughters, Gay and Janet, during that summer of 1937 did much to heal the scars of *Floodlight* and enhance my passion for the opera, which had been developing during the preceding year in London with visits to Covent Garden, sometimes with my friend, Philip Zorab, and sometimes with my dearly loved and absolutely favourite girl, Rose Paget, to Lady Cunard's box.

For me there is little to beat the feeling of the opera-house, that excited murmur of voices against the sound of the orchestra tuning up. Smartly dressed people, a sudden wave of laughter, followed by a quick glissando on the harp. An F sharp from a trumpet. A flutter up and down the scale from a flute, champagne glasses clinking in the crush bar . . . then the hush and the house lights dimmed down, the ripple of applause for the leader, then for the maestro. Baton raised. Footlights up. Overture . . . curtain up . . . magic.

The smart people in the boxes at Covent Garden today are no longer Lady Cunard's guests, or the Londonderrys' or the Angleseys', or the Hambledens', as it used to be. The Royal Box is probably Shell's tonight and will be ICI's tomorrow. The Prudential Assurance may have the box opposite, like they have shooting in Hampshire and fishing on the Test. Or is it the Midland Bank? The guests in the boxes are friends of the managing director, or of the chairman of the board. But the opera goes on with its new sponsors and patrons, firms rather than music-loving patricians. And thank God for the firms. Big business is the new patron of the arts and sport. Without it, disaster.

And so in many languages the opera goes on. Butterfly slits her throat behind that screen, Tosca stabs Scarpia for every successive generation, Carmen waggles her hips in New York, in Rome, in London; Don Giovanni descends into hell in Vienna and Sussex and people still queue for tickets and find their musical ecstasy and uplift in the opera houses of the world.

I suppose the flame was lit inside me in childhood, for the very first tune my mother ever played for me on the drawing-room piano at Norfolk Square, when Nanny brought us down after tea for the usual half-hour devoted to the children, was not 'Little Bo-Peep' or 'Jack and Jill' but 'One Fine Day' from the opera *Madame Butterfly*.

Mama, I remember, told me about the man who composed it and how she had sat next to him at a dinner-party in Paris; and what a clever man he was. All that ran off me like water off a duck's back. I just loved the melody and hummed it on my way upstairs to the nursery. It was only later on, when opera grabbed me totally, that I realized my mother had actually met and known the great Giacomo Puccini.

When I was fourteen, Mama gave me Gustav Kobbé's *Opera Book*. Later she showed me a faded visiting card which she kept in a glass-framed picture. On one side of the card was the printed name of a gentleman called M. Rene Escudier with an address in the Avenue Foch, Paris. On the reverse side, the blank side, were a few bars of music in a scrawled hand and a signature, Giacomo Puccini, March 1909. The music was a short passage from *Butterfly*.

It seems that when Mother was a seventeen-year-old American girl studying in Paris, she dined at someone's house and found herself seated between this M. Escudier and Puccini, who was already a great celebrity. When between courses my mother daringly asked the famous composer for his autograph, Puccini acceded but had nothing to write on; so Mama turned to M. Escudier on her left, who promptly volunteered one of his visiting cards. Puccini scribbled down four or five bars of his immortal opera, Mama put the card in her reticule and that was that.

Puccini became my number one opera composer and still is. I have seen and enjoyed countless other works in the opera house: all the Verdis, Wagners – the easy ones – Massenet, Rossini, Mozart at Glyndebourne, one-offs like Charpentier's *Louise*, Richard Strauss, Bizet; all magic, all superb. But for sheer emo-

tional ecstasy, Puccini wins for me. I can still see that little handful of his operas over and over again and never tire of them. I
know every note of *Il Tabarro,* of *Tosca,* of *Turandot.* I seriously
believe *La Bohème* to be the greatest piece of music drama ever
staged. I am obsessed with the man's genius for melody and for
the welding together of theatrical drama with sung music. His
operas are terrific 'theatre', packed with moments that send
shudders down the spine however many times you see them. The
first entrance of Scarpia into the church in *Tosca*; the Bonze's
sudden appearance in *Butterfly*; then, of course, all those soaring
arias. It's very amusing to me how musical snobs look down their
noses at Puccini, simply because he is so damned good that he is
still sung and hummed all over the world. He is far too popular and
too successful to be acceptable to the musical élite. They tend to
dismiss him as a 'facile tunesmith' or a sugary romantic operetta
writer on a par with Lehar or Romberg or Ivor Novello.

But people who really know music rate him very high. I once
heard Beecham tearing apart the bogus connoisseurs who belittle
Puccini. Sir Thomas was asked on the radio why he respected
Puccini so much. Beecham replied: 'Because he knew his job backwards and he wrote damn good tunes. That's good enough for me.'

Once on holiday in Italy I went on a pilgrimage to the Torre del
Lago Puccini, near Viareggio in Tuscany. Here Puccini's famous
weekend villa on the lake, where he used to go duck-flighting, has
been preserved as a museum and memorial to the maestro.
Puccini's piano was there with his pencil and india rubber and bits
of scribbled music on manuscript. You could almost see him sitting
there fuming at those poor bullied librettists, Giacosa and Illica,
a cigarette in his mouth, pounding out the great chords of *Tosca*
or *Manon Lescaut* or *Il Tabarro* and demanding fresh coffee from
his devoted housekeeper.

In the porch of Puccini's villa you can still see his rubber waders,
decoy ducks, guns, cartridge bags and various walking sticks. How
strange for a man to be lying out in a punt on a lake at first light
waiting for the duck to come over his gun; and then, an hour later,
for that same man to be at his piano composing the tenderest little
arias for *Turandot* and *Butterfly;* then speeding away in the train
or in his own early motor car for a meeting in Milan with
Toscanini or the directors of La Scala or with Ricordi, his pub-
lishers.

Such a colourful, romantic, fascinating figure and such a musician. Yet, for all my nights of enchantment at Puccini operas, the greatest experience I ever had in an opera house was provided for me by Richard Strauss at the Salzburg Festival in that aforementioned summer of 1937, the last season to be held there before the Anschluss. It was a very tense time, most Austrians knowing full well that Hitler would soon swallow up their country. It was also a very exciting and 'starry' season. All the great singers were there that year and Toscanini was conducting. The audiences were international and every night the opera house was packed with film stars, millionaires, diplomats, and society people.

The performance I can never forget was one of Hugo von Hofmannsthal's and Richard Strauss's lovely *Der Rosenkavalier* with a cast which, in that year, seemed absolutely staggering: Lotte Lehmann, Elizabeth Schumann, Jarmila Novotna, Emanuel List as Ochs and the conductor was Hans Knappertsbusch from Munich.

The effect of that glorious trio of female voices, '*Hab mir's gelobt ihr Lieb zu haben*', with its slowly building, key-changing climax, sung by such a cast lifted me right out of my seat and up into heaven. I've never experienced such total ecstasy from a sound before and probably never will again. After all I was only twenty-one and at a most impressionable age. For that experience I shall always be grateful to France Margesson for having me to stay in her chalet, where I recall I shared a room with Laurence Whistler, brother of Rex, because we were a houseful.

From Salzburg I flew back to Croydon by Lufthansa in the company of Priscilla Bibesco, who had been in the party. We landed, as one did in those days, about four times to refuel: Munich, Frankfurt, Cologne, Amsterdam. . . . Priscilla was a good friend and we'd been out quite a bit in London. She lived with her distinguished grandmother, Lady Oxford and Asquith, at her house in Bedford Square. Margot Asquith's son 'Puffin' also lived there and I thus came to know him long before I ever went into films. I recall sitting with Priscilla late at night after the theatre in the study at Bedford Square, sipping a nightcap and whispering sweet nothings to her but faltering as my eye caught a marble bust of the former Liberal Prime Minister looking down at me with a cold expression of disapproval.

Lady Oxford had been a formidable character in British society for some decades, and continued to be so right into old age. My last encounter with that great figure of her time was an evening in 1941 during the London blitz, when I elected to spend my forty-eight hours leave at the Savoy. She was dining with seven or eight elderly men in the Grill, whose huge plate glass windows were walled up against the bombs. I was dining alone and listening to Carroll Gibbons, who was playing in the Grill. Seeing Lady Oxford, I went over to say hullo and she insisted on my joining her party. The eight elderly men at her table proved to be the entire Netherlands Government in exile. She introduced me to them all by name without a moment's hesitation.

Later, at her invitation, I went down to talk to her in the shelter under the Savoy, where she held court every night throughout the blitz in woolly combinations and a hair net.

— EIGHT —

I Plunge into Show Business,
Europe Plunges into War

In the autumn of 1937 I took the most important step of my life.

During the rehearsals for *Floodlight* I had met, admired and made friends with the press representative for the show, an ex-*Daily Express* show business columnist called Robert Ellison. Sitting with him day after day in the Saville, Bob Ellison had pointed out much that was going wrong with the show and through him I had learned quite a lot about the theatre business generally.

He had just formed with Dennis van Thal, now a very notable theatrical agent, a small firm to handle publicity and represent a few artistes and writers; and, if suitable properties and backing could be found, to present straight plays and musical shows. After a couple of lunches at the Café Royal and a cheque from me for £250 goodwill money, I joined them.

It was just what I was looking for: an opening into show business that would look to my family like a 'proper occupation'; an office to go to in the mornings by tube with an umbrella and hat. Somewhere to work at a desk.

We had a small office off Regent Street and at first it was the publicity side that prospered through Bob's Fleet Street contacts. One of the firm's clients was Harold Holt, the concert impresario, and one of my first assignments with Ellison, Shaughnessy and van Thal Ltd was to attend a press reception at the Piccadilly Hotel for Rachmaninoff, who was in London to give a Harold Holt concert at the Albert Hall. I shall never forget shaking hands with this thin, gaunt old man and noting his long, lean and, as I recall, trembling fingers.

After a month or two Dennis van Thal left us to join Christopher Mann's considerably larger agency, so Bob Ellison and I 'soldiered on' (an unfortunate phrase as it turned out) into 1938, a year of crisis and foreboding as the war clouds gathered over Europe.

We handled the publicity for Emlyn Williams' wonderful play *The Corn is Green* at the Duchess, which afforded me the opportunity of getting to know briefly that brilliant and witty Welsh master of the theatre; and we presented, most unwisely, a totally incomprehensible 'avant-garde' Danish fantasy called *The Melody That Got Lost* by Kjeld Abell at the Phoenix. I was talked into this project by Denis Freeman who had staged *Floodlight*. In the event I actually wrote a scene or two for the English version plus a bit of music for it.

The first night of *The Melody* at the Phoenix Theatre in 1938 was a more than usually glittering and fashionable affair with three duchesses in the audience, many ambassadors, Mr C. B. Cochran *and* Noël Coward. Margaret Rutherford scored a minor triumph in the play and Dorothy Hyson was enchanting. We also had Esmond Knight in the cast and Viola Tree. But the *Daily Mail* notice was headed 'Actors Get Lost in a Symbolic Fog' and we were off within a fortnight.

Undaunted, Bob and I became interested in a new play called *Power and Glory* by Karel Capek, the Czech author with his brother of *The Insect Play* and *R.U.R.*. Oscar Homolka wished to appear in this then topical mid-European drama about a dictator, who contracts a lethal disease, and a radical doctor, who refuses to cure him unless he disarms his country and rejects war.

The *scène à faire* of this play was inevitably the final confrontation between dictator and doctor. Mr Homolka, however, elected to play both parts himself thus destroying the confrontation scene and so the play, which in spite of a distinguished cast including Felix Aylmer, C. V. France, Noel Howlett and others, entered the Savoy Theatre on the Tuesday and left the following Saturday fortnight.

The time had now come for Bob and me to do something we felt we knew more about and to make some money. So in the early summer of 1938, we signed a contract with the Eastbourne Corporation to produce a summer show at the Winter Garden Theatre. We knew the Winter Garden was something of a white elephant and that Clarkson Rose's famous summer show *Twinkle*, which always cleaned up wherever it went, was booked to occupy the Pier Theatre that summer season – stiff opposition indeed.

However, we were keen to have a go and our colleague Denis Freeman was eager to produce the show. We'd all have a splendid working holiday on the South Coast. In order not to clash with the rather corny and traditional *Twinkle* we decided to be clever and present a 'West End Revue by the Sea', building it round Charles Heslop, a versatile revue star and definitely West End, and using a shifting repertoire of good revue material by authors like Herbert Farjeon, A. P. Herbert, Ronald Jeans, Diana Morgan and Robert MacDermott, Eric Maschwitz and others. The Eastbourne Corporation pundits, after watching rehearsals, asked us nervously if our show might not be a touch too sophisticated for the holiday-makers. 'Oh, no,' we answered, filled with confidence, 'they'll love it.'

I'm afraid the Corporation's fears were well founded. We did some fairly good weeks, depending on the material in the show and the weather; but, all in all, while the blasted *Twinkle* with its awful crinoline and poke-bonneted Valentine ensembles, baritones singing 'Trees' and 'The Road to the Isles' and dreadful stand-up comics cracking bad but wholesome jokes, played to capacity throughout the season, *The Pleasure of Your Company* as we called our show, tottered on and on, seldom clearing its running costs. In my enthusiasm for revue and having inherited a bit of money under my grandfather's trust, I had foolishly underwritten the operation. So the summer of 1938 cost me over a thousand pounds. But I enjoyed every moment of it. The company were delightful, Betty Hare, Cyril Wells, Bert Brownhill, Leonard Hayes, Pamela Foster, the ballerina, and some other dishy little girls, not to mention Charles Heslop himself, such a nice man and quite incrediby fit and nimble for his years.

I wrote a certain number of sketches and lyrics and a little music for *The Pleasure of Your Company* and so did Bob Ellison. So, when the Eastbourne venture ended, leaving us bloody nearly broke but unbowed, we spent the following winter and the spring of 1939 preparing the intimate revue to end all intimate revues. We were determined to take London by storm with a really clever, funny, witty, beautiful little show, written and composed entirely by ourselves. I had dreamed up a title, *'Fiddlesticks'*, which I thought a good one, and we felt with the lessons learned the preceding summer in Eastbourne, we knew it all.

In the early summer, about May, of 1939, I began to try to raise the backing for *'Fiddlesticks'*. I again went to a few of my well-heeled, theatre-loving friends and somehow managed to collect all the money we needed. One of these generous 'angel' friends of mine was Terence O'Neil, who years later became Prime Minister of Northern Ireland and who, if Paisley and his extreme Loyalists had left him alone, might well have pushed civil rights and reforms for the Ulster Catholics through the Stormont Parliament and saved the Province from bloodshed. Anyway, the *'Fiddlesticks'* finance was raised and we were off.

The Whitehall Theatre was empty and looking for an autumn production at very reasonable terms. So Bob and I went to have a look and realized there was no orchestra pit in the place. With a revue you must have somewhere, if only room for two pianos. And we were planning for a small orchestra. So, at a cost of about £300 we had an orchestra pit built into the Whitehall Theatre. As the summer wore on, everyone became more and more certain that war was inevitable. I felt sick in the stomach and very torn. I was on the Royal Army Reserve of Officers and might soon be called up. Half of me wanted to get out of the whole revue commitment. At home in St James's Palace all the dinner-table talk was of Hitler's unreasonable demands on Poland, about Danzig, the Polish corridor, Colonel Beck. And yet, the show had to go on. What else could one do?

Bob and I finished most of the material and started to cast our revue. Charles Heslop joined us again, as did Betty Hare and Pam Foster. Also Edward Cooper, the clever cabaret entertainer, and Angus Menzies, a dark handsome young man, well-known in society, who looked like a god and sang like a tenor. With the theatre and casting fixed, Bob and I flew off to Monte Carlo to get some sun and polish up our material for the show. We stayed at the Hotel Terminus, which at the time was housing the de Basil Ballet de Monte Carlo. So Bob and I spent our mornings typing out sketches and lyrics on the flat roof of the hotel, hopelessly distracted by Toumanova, Riabouchinska, Baronova and other such lovely creatures in black practice costumes, perfecting their arabesques and entrechats under our very noses. We swam and dined at the Sporting Club and chatted up one or two members of a troupe of English showgirls who were there for the 1939 season.

The whole atmosphere of Monte Carlo during that July and August of 1939 was dreamlike, unreal, somehow almost macabre.

The place was packed with rich people, smart cars, big yachts; the band on the Sporting Club terrace played the Cole Porter songs from *Leave It To Me* which was all the rage in New York. One number in particular will always evoke that fateful, dramatic summer for me. It seemed to fill the air every evening . . . 'Come On and Sing, My Heart'.

Everybody danced and swam and gambled and made love and nobody mentioned war. But in our hearts we all knew it was just over the horizon.

In mid-August Bob and I packed our cases and returned to London to start our rehearsals. By the last week in August *'Fiddlesticks'* was beginning to take shape. I was pleased with my music, largely thanks to Elsie April, Noël Coward's and C. B. Cochran's musical director, who had also arranged Beverley Nichols' songs for *Floodlight,* and was making my stuff sound marvellous. She was a musical genius. A small birdlike woman in a felt hat, looking like a little school music teacher, she would sit at the upright piano on the stage performing miracles with my roughly-hewn melodies and harmonies in E flat and A flat. Elsie could sight-read a number and transpose it into another key as she played, improving the harmony and general flow of the piece. And if, through sheer musical illiteracy like mine, you got yourself into the wrong key by developing a too elaborate melody line, Elsie April could run you up a little passage of the most cunning and devious notation and progression, which brought you back into E flat or whatever it was and nobody ever noticed. She knocked out wonderful intros and bridges and knew just about all there was to be known about enriching with good harmony a mediocre top-line.

At last came the fateful day. Friday, 1 September, 1939. Things were already about as critical as they could be. Ribbentrop was about to sign a pact with Stalin. But there was still no reason to abandon our revue. We were not yet at war.

It was a clear, fine, autumn morning, as I walked along the Mall from St James's towards the Admiralty Arch headed for the stage door of the Whitehall. As I walked, I was wondering whether our cast was strong enough for us to survive tepid notices and recalling how some months earlier I had talked to Rex Harrison about the possibility of his doing our revue. I had met Harrison through Iris Mountbatten, who was a friend and fan. He was already a big star playing Leo in *Design for Living* at the Haymarket, so I was amazed when he took my entirely tentative suggestion quite seriously. He said he'd always wanted to do a revue. But what an actor says he'd love to do and what his agent in the cold light of day will let him do is another matter. Rex's agent had soon put his foot down on that little scheme and we had pressed ahead with Charles Heslop. With these reflections, I now arrived at the stage door of the Whitehall. The stage-door keeper had a portable radio in his cubby hole and from it was emanating a news bulletin. 'The balloon's gone up, sir,' said the old chap, as I passed him. 'He's marched into Poland early this morning.' And that was it. I swallowed hard, croaked something silly like: 'I thought he would,' and swaying slightly from the shock of the sudden certainty of war, I entered the dark theatre.

On stage the cast were standing huddled into groups, talking anxiously. Two of the girls were in tears. Bob was there, looking stunned. Bill Newman, our General Manager, was on the phone to someone, probably – with his usual foresight – cancelling the wigs before it was too late.

Bob and I consulted hastily in a corner and asked the cast to remain in the theatre while we made some more telephone calls. I had to check my call-up. Half-way up the aisle we met Elsie April coming in. She'd been working with Noël Coward over at the Haymarket on the musical arrangements for *Present Laughter* and *This Happy Breed*. 'Noël's closing down at once,' she told us. 'He's just spoken to Anthony Eden on the phone, who says war is inevitable so he's cancelled rehearsals. What are *you* going to do?' Bob and I looked at each other. I think we both realized at once that for Noël Coward to cancel a production things must be hopeless. So we decided on the spot to do likewise. I made a short speech to the cast in which I said that I would have to report to Wellington Barracks as a reservist but that Bob was willing to carry on. However, I said, it seemed most unlikely that we should not be at war by Monday morning and, since it was Friday and we were all a bit upset and confused, we'd better disperse for the weekend and see what happened.

More tears from the girls. Charles Heslop, who'd been in the 1914-18 War, declared that he was ready to fight the Hun again, if they'd take him, and swept out of the theatre.

Everyone dispersed quietly and I went back with Bob to his flat and later home to St James's. That afternoon I reported to HQ

Grenadier Guards at Wellington Barracks. I was mobilized. *'Fiddlesticks'* for me was dead.

During the war – for my troop shows – and afterwards I used up some of my old *'Fiddlesticks'* material. It all played well, so who knows? The show might have succeeded. But the real tragedy was that within a week or two of 3 September, the 'phoney war' set in and every single theatre in London opened up to capacity business. 1939 was a boom winter in the West End. Everything and anything with music and laughter ran and ran. If *we'd* opened, *'Fiddlesticks'* might have run for years.

As it was the Whitehall Theatre fell into the hands of a blonde lady with a quiet voice and a well developed body called Phyllis Dixey, who stripped for the troops over the years that followed, accompanied by an orchestra playing in *my* pit.

Later in the blitz winter of 1941, all the scenery and costumes for *'Fiddlesticks'* which had been stored in a warehouse in South London, were destroyed by incendiaries, uninsured. Then in 1944, soon after our Grenadier Group had captured the famous bridge at Nijmegen, Bob Ellison's mother wrote to tell me her son had been killed in action quite near to where we were. And I never knew he'd joined up. Bob was a big influence in my life and taught me a lot about plays and people. He more than anyone showed me the other side of life than my own rather sheltered and privileged background.

Although I contributed to revues after the war, *'Fiddlesticks'* was the only time I got near to a whole show of my own and Bob was the nearest I came to a Gilbert and Sullivan or Rodgers and Hammerstein partnership with anyone.

It was my revue writing that first convinced me that I could and would eventually write a full-length play; but I have always retained a love of the black-out sketch, the witty lyric and the point number. While I was fighting with the Guards Armoured Division in Germany in 1944, I heard that one of my old *'Fiddlesticks'* sketches had been put into a revue called *New Faces* at the Comedy. It was called 'Pick Up' and concerned a young man, who has brought a girl back to his flat in order to seduce her, turned down the lights, put Delius on the gramophone and poured the champagne. She is very dense and silly and doesn't realize what he is up to. She asks if she may phone her mother and has a long, vapid conversation with Mum while the young man's ardour cools off.

The original cast was Bill Fraser and the talented Betty Ann Davies. It was later done dozens of times all over the place and once, I believe, was performed in an ENSA show in Italy by John Gielgud and Vivien Leigh.

Another sketch I wrote, 'Non Compos Mentis', appeared after the war in a big revue at the Cambridge Theatre called *Sauce Piquante*. In it Norman Wisdom appeared as a lunatic in a railway carriage with Douglas Byng as, of all things, a general. Bob Monkhouse played a porter and the sketch was announced by Audrey Hepburn, who was in the chorus of the show.

One of my songs for *'Fiddlesticks'* was a point number called 'The Oldest Chorus Boy in London', which was very camp indeed and was later sung in a revue called *Up and Doing* by Cyril Ritchard, who also made a record of it; and later by Walter Crisham. There was also a rather obscene lyric called 'My Pet Perversion' about a society woman who secretly scribbles graffiti on the posters in the Underground. This was admirably performed in Ciro's and elsewhere after the war by Hermione Baddeley, who succeeded in making the number sound even ruder than it really was.

But I'd have preferred to present all that material in *'Fiddlesticks'* at the Whitehall. Damn the war.

— NINE —

Into Battle with the Grenadiers

Since my stepfather had been a Grenadier, it was natural that after Sandhurst I should enter the First Regiment of Foot-Guards. As recounted earlier, I did not, in fact, enter any regiment in 1934; but I had been persuaded after the Munich Crisis of 1938 to place my name on a reserve list of potential officers and to do some peace-time training at Wellington Barracks. On two evenings a week I and a number of my contemporaries, hot foot from the City or wherever in bowler hats and carrying umbrellas, would be chased up and down the parade ground by a Coldstream drill-sergeant to howls of laughter from the less patriotic or perceptive of His Majesty's subjects, peering at us through the railings of Birdcage Walk. When war did come in September 1939, I was called up at once by the Grenadiers and sent straight back again to Sandhurst, the establishment from which I had resigned four years earlier. The Royal Military College had meanwhile become an OCTU and the course was short and not very sweet.

I was on weekend leave from the wretched place once when the King and Queen came for a pre-lunch Sunday drink at St James's. I'd had a curious experience during the preceding week, while cycling through Camberley, dressed, as we OCTU cadets were, in battledress and a khaki fore-and-aft cap with a square patch of white cloth sewn on to the side of it. This was supposed to denote 'OCTU Cadet, training to be an officer, not to be confused with ordinary soldier'.

As I bicycled towards two civilian girls pushing prams along the pavement, they nudged each other and giggled. And when I rode past them I heard one say to the other: 'Coo, look at him. He's got a price on his head.'

74

My brother Tom, who was also at home that Sunday, recounted this experience of mine to the King. I have never seen a man laugh so much. His Majesty literally doubled up and roared with mirth until the tears streamed down his face.

One of our Company at the OCTU was Lord Jellicoe, son of the Admiral, who was possessed of a rather larger than usual head. Since the clothing store was unable to provide a khaki fore-and-aft cap to fit him, he was allowed to wear instead his own checkered cloth-cap with his battledress. Thus on parade George Jellicoe resembled a Red Chinese engineer, as he took his turn at drilling the rest of us on the lawn by the lake. When he shouted, 'Company by the left quick march,' we marched obediently off towards the lake. When, now at some distance, we heard George cry out 'About turn,' Brian Johnston muttered, 'Pretend we can't hear him.' So we all marched beautifully in step with relentless precision towards the lake like the Gadarene swine and nearly went in before the drill-sergeant took over and turned us round.

By February 1940 I was an ensign in the Grenadiers, proud and eager, with the training battalion at Windsor, where I had my first taste of actually commanding men. It's a funny feeling when for the first time you shout a command such as 'Quick march' or 'Stand easy' to a squad of real soldiers, not just one's colleagues on an officers' training course. When you get your first officer's uniform and cap and face a real platoon, it's a bit like the thrill of getting into the cab of an enormous powerful lorry, switching on the engine and engaging gear. In a lorry, you let in the clutch and find to your amazement that it actually moves forward. You press the brake and it stops. So with your first platoon. You say the magic words 'Quick march' and thirty large, tall and independent-minded Guardsmen, grown men with wives and children and the right to vote, actually do what you say. Shout 'Halt' and they stop. You wonder why they should . . . for you? Well, it's your uniform, your rank, isn't it? You represent the sovereign; it's His Majesty's Commission that you hold. So they halt and stand there like robots, until you start them off again. It's a strange feeling of power – at first. Later you reflect that if they didn't stop, when you shouted 'Halt', you'd have a mutiny on your hands and you, not they, would be in dead trouble. In the end, you realize that discipline in the army is a conspiracy, a sort of tacit agreement by both sides, officers, warrant officers and men, to act out a sort of charade, to play together a kind of game, because it all works and, if it's done properly, everyone feels good and safe and nobody wants to swap roles.

My time at Windsor spanned the so-called 'phoney war' period of 1939-40 and life in the mess was almost unchanged from peacetime. All the formalities and traditions of the regiment were drummed into us newly-gazetted subalterns by the adjutant. We were instructed to call all officers bar the CO by their Christian names when off-parade; we were shown the correct angle to wear our caps while breakfasting in the mess – a curious old custom of the Brigade of Guards; we learned the various duties of the picquet officer, which included turning out the guard last thing at night. This was a hazardous operation after compulsorily sitting over the port in the mess for anything up to three hours, recording on a sheet of paper the number of glasses taken by each dining-in officer from a seemingly bottomless decanter; and there were the mysteries of mounting guard at Windsor Castle.

The latter chore was quite exciting. I enjoyed marching along the terraces and battlements at night, the drummer leading the way with a swinging lantern, the Sergeant of the Guard and the relief sentries following, ready to change over. It was good theatre.

The actual ceremony of taking over the guard occurred daily outside the guardroom opposite St George's Chapel and was a simplified version of what thousands of tourists watch outside Buckingham Palace every day.

I only did one Castle Guard at Windsor but it gave me an anxious moment. I was relieving Martin McLaren, later the Conservative Member for Bristol North-West, who was the Officer of the Old Guard. There comes a moment in the ceremonial drill when the Officer of the New Guard (me) has to take two paces forward and extend his hand to the Officer of the Old Guard (Martin) in order to receive the keys of the guardroom.

I advanced, banged my boots down hard to halt and shot out my right hand. Instead of the expected cold metal of a bunch of keys in my waiting palm, I felt a little tickle, as though a small insect had somehow settled there. Then I twigged. Martin had forgotten to bring the keys on parade. The tickle was his way of informing me of his omission. I closed my fist smartly and, with meaningful resolve, took two paces to the rear. The parade continued. Somehow the keys reached the New Guard before the Old

Guard marched away to the band down the hill and back to Victoria Barracks.

We did a little field training in Windsor Park as a concession to the fact that all Europe was 'technically' at war during that cold winter. One frosty night in February 1940 my company defended the Copper Horse from a mounted assault by a squadron of the Household Cavalry from Combermere Barracks.

As the elegant young officers of the Blues and Life Guards galloped at the head of their respective troops against our entrenched and impregnable positions in the bracken at the foot of the famous statue of George II, we replied by waving football rattles to represent Bren gun fire. The night was filled with shouts of 'After you, Charles' and 'Corporal Major, I think the Duke of Roxburgh's had a fall. Go and tell Lord Arthur will you?' It sounded more like a day with the Cottesmore than a military night exercise. After a time, a stout major with the white armband of an umpire cantered up with a cigar in his mouth and told us we had successfully repulsed the Uhlans' attack. The 'stunt' – as Guardsmen always call an exercise – ended with a sort of nocturnal picnic of sandwiches and cherry brandy for the officers and hot soup for the men, much social gossip and some ragging about to keep warm. Then we all went back to the comfort of Victoria Barracks for a hot bath and a game of bridge.

Within a matter of weeks the German Panzer divisions were thundering across France and Belgium, smashing the French armies and driving the BEF into the sea. One of the perquisites of being Officer of the Guard at Windsor was a standing invitation to dine with the Dean of Windsor at his house in the precincts. Dean Bailey was a gay old fellow and very good company. As a close friend of Ivor Novello's he was much interested in the stage. This made conversation easier for me and we talked at dinner of theatrical matters to take our minds off the ghastly news of that afternoon that France was on the verge of collapse. Thus it was in the Dean of Windsor's drawing-room that I heard Winston Churchill's historic broadcast announcing the surrender of the French armies, Britain's resolve to fight on and his desperate offer to the French people of joint-citizenship with Britain, if they would stay in the war.

In the years that followed 1940 I served continually with the 1st Battalion of the Grenadier Guards, in training and in battle, a period of my life at which I shall always look back with pride and warmth. My war was, largely through the lengthy transformation of my battalion with several other units of the Footguards into the Guards Armoured Division, only about a quarter dangerous and three-quarters boring or amusing. I did not go into battle until July 1944 but that was quite soon enough for me.

Much has been written by abler pens than mine about action in war but since my father was killed in the trenches in 1916 and I took part briefly in and survived the Second World War, I feel I cannot by-pass the ugly subject altogether. I think I can best sum up war, as I knew it, by recounting one vivid and typical impression I have never been able to erase from my mind. It was in Normandy, July 1944. We were locked in battle with a German Panzer Corps in an area of the Bocage country not far from Caen. I had occasion to pass in my armoured scout car up and down a very dusty, dangerous stretch of road between our Bn. Headquarters, concealed in some woods, and one of our forward motor companies, who were in contact with the enemy. The whole area was devastated: dead cows, burning tanks, telegraph poles and wires down, shell craters. You had to drive like hell along that stretch of open road to reach cover before the mortar bombs and shells came crashing down, for it was overlooked by German artillery and mortar units.

Midway along this deadly piece of road was an overturned armoured car of the 12th Lancers, which had gone up on a mine some days earlier and was burnt out. The mutilated body of the young subaltern who had commanded it was dangling head-down, half out of the turret, the arms almost touching the road. To stop and bury the poor chap would have been suicidal, for the verge of the road was mined and the dust sent up by one's vehicle would have brought down the shells. So the wrecked armoured car and its luckless occupant remained untouched on that road for three or four more hot, sunbaked days.

Each time I raced down the road past this gruesome sight, the subaltern's body had disintegrated just a little further; soon flies were crawling over it. The blackened face seemed to wither and you caught an unpleasant smell. When, after a day or two, we moved on out of that area, the brewed-up armoured car was still there on that stretch of French road, a burnt-out hulk, its occupant putrefying further in the sun; it was an obscene mess of charred flesh, shattered bone and flies, that had once been a proud and gallant young officer. . . .

My mind envisaged as I drove away from the sight, a brave little gathering in some village church in England. The young officer's parents, grave, dressed in black, tear-stained but proud. His sister, on compassionate leave from the Wrens, kneeling stunned in her pew. The rector, an old friend of the family, heartbroken, trying to get out the words, 'This boy we all knew and loved, Ronnie, who died so bravely for his country.' I saw the family plaque on the church wall; soon the new name would be added, carved in the pure white marble: 'Ronald, only son of . . . killed in action, Normandy, July 1944.' The neat little Wren in her imagination would see her brother fall, a bullet clean through his heart, carried into a wood by his comrades to die quietly under the trees and later to be buried with a wooden cross beside a cool stream.

But I saw war at first hand. I saw what, mercifully, that imaginary family never saw. I saw their Ronnie as he finished up. An obscene twisted human trunk hanging bent and blackened out of the turret of a wrecked armoured car, rotting in the sun, at the mercy of the flies and the putrefaction . . . and *that* is war. And as the vision of that young officer hanging dead from his armoured car still haunts me, so does the memory of one awful wet, depressing and tragic night in 1944 after the first day of what is now studied on staff college courses as Operation Goodwood. It was not only the night after my own baptism of fire in battle but an evening when the first ever casualty reports for the Guards Armoured Division came in and friends were known to have been killed that afternoon. One such was Rex Whistler.

Some experts have pronounced Rex more a brilliant 'decorator' than an artist. I suppose this slightly condescending attitude to his work derives from the fact that he designed so many book jackets, programmes for gala performances, sets for plays and romantic murals on the walls of friends' houses. These murals with the most gorgeous vistas of seas and hills and palaces and villas and elegant people are reminiscent to me of the work of Claude Lorrain. Furthermore Rex never wrote a letter to a friend without including a wealth of witty illustration. He was a compulsive illustrator.

I suppose his style was essentially eighteenth-century Romantic and there are times when I feel Rex ought to have lived in that century. He would have been in his element.

Of course, like the great painters of bygone days, Rex Whistler was very much a patronized artist. He became, quite early in his career, the most fashionable, lionized young painter and designer in London. Many of the great collectors and noble families took him up, mainly those with taste and an appreciation of the arts: the Manners, Pagets, Cecils, Wellesleys, Herberts and many others.

But Rex was utterly unspoilt. Much has been said elsewhere of his eternally youthful, puckish charm, his enthusiasm, his generosity. I must confine myself to my own experience of him.

I first met Rex through Rose Maclaren, a daughter of Lord and Lady Anglesey, whom, as I have said, I loved dearly as Rose Paget and have gone on loving dearly for forty years. One of my earliest memories of Rex is going with Rose to a party he gave at his house in Fitzroy Square to celebrate the marriage of his talented brother, Laurence, to the beautiful actress Jill Furse, who died so tragically young. I met Rex frequently after that around London and staying at Plas Newydd with the Anglesey family, where he was a semi-permanent guest for a year or two as he worked on his now famous mural in the dining-room there.

When war broke out and I joined the Grenadiers, rumour started to circulate that Rex Whistler was seeking a commission in the Brigade of Guards. The idea of Rex as a Guards officer was almost comic in a way – one could envisage the kind of Guards officer he would draw, a lovely caricature with monocle and guardee moustache. But all sorts of unlikely people were donning uniform in those days and it wasn't long before a story was going the rounds of White's and Bucks to the effect that Rex Whistler had been to see Colonel 'Cheeko' Leatham, the fiery and formidable lieutenant-colonel commanding the Welsh Guards, whose officers were by then being drawn from a wide range of civilian activities. Evidently, when Rex reported to Colonel Leatham in the orderly room and was asked what he did for a living, Rex replied that he was an artist. To which Colonel Leatham is alleged to have said: 'Never mind, if you join us, you'll find a fellah called Elwes down at the depot. They tell me he's quite handy with a paintbrush too.' So Rex found himself an ensign in the Welsh Guards along with a fellow artist, Simon Elwes.

The regiment boasted a number of other distinguished, creative people among its officers before the war ended, notably novelist

Richard Llewellyn, actor Anthony Bushell and the historian and biographer Kenneth Rose.

During the long training period in England of the Guards Armoured Division, I saw quite a bit of Rex, for the 2nd Bn. Welsh Guards were in the Division and we were from time to time stationed near each other. I spent one dreadfully cold night with him stranded in the fog on the Yorkshire wolds out of petrol and miserable in a P/U, a sort of officers' shooting brake. Needless to say, he was very good company to be marooned with. We were on our way back from a party at Sledmere given by Virginia Sykes and as we shivered under an army blanket in the back of that wretched vehicle, we went through all the people who'd been at the party and discussed who was in love with whom. Just like two old nannies, gossiping on a park bench. It wasn't until four in the morning that I managed to stop a truck, get petrol, drop Rex back at Pocklington, where he was billeted, and proceed to Ampleforth where I was installed.

After dining with me once in our Mess at Piddlehinton Camp in Dorset, Rex came over to my Nissen hut for a chat and a glass of port; always having busy hands, he took a piece of chinagraph pencil from my map-case and idly drew on the wall over my bed the most charming nude of a young girl with one stocking on. I photographed the drawing, because anything Rex drew was even then likely to be of future interest and importance. When we left the camp, handing over to a Polish unit, I wrote under the drawing: 'Please do not destroy. This was painted by Rex Whistler. March 1942.' I've no idea what happened to it, but I did give the photograph of it to Laurence, his brother, who I am certain has that at least safely preserved.

In 1943, the Division was stationed near Thetford in Norfolk. It wasn't long before Rex took me over to lunch at Breccles, Venetia Montagu's lovely Queen Anne house, and over lunch talked Venetia into letting us give a party there. She agreed to lend her house and what staff she had. We made arrangements to pool our rations, supply the drink and arrange for large numbers of wives and girl friends to come down by train to be billeted for the night with other friends nearby. It was a mammoth operation, similar to those peacetime balls in the great houses, where neighbours gave dinner and house-parties to accommodate the ball guests from London. That such an event could take place in East

Anglia in 1943 is almost shaming. But it did. I got landed by Rex with most of the organizing of girls and billets, while he busied himself decorating Breccles for the occasion. He drew vast, orgiastic posters of Bacchus, of obscene and obese satyrs and slim fauns and nymphs to adorn the walls of the drawing-room and hall. We prayed for good weather and got it. The party took place on a warm, starry June night and the atmosphere of that beautiful house with its magnificent rose garden and tilting yard alive with music and laughter and filled with lovely people was something to be remembered.

It was, I suppose, one of a number of 'Waterloo Balls'. Every time we had a glamorous party during those last months before D-Day, we used to look at each other and say: 'We shall never see this again.' Or 'This is *our* Duchess of Richmond's Ball.' It became a cliché. For some of us, such as Rex Whistler, it was indeed a 'last fling'.

The last time I ever saw Rex was on the morning of Operation Goodwood, the big armoured break-out from the Caen bridgehead, an enterprise which went all wrong. It was the Guards Armoured Division's first big battle of the war. All our tanks were lined up in huge columns in a cornfield outside Bayeux. It was dawn on a July day in 1944. Lovely weather. I was driving in my scout car down the column to visit one of our units and happened to pass the 2nd Bn. Welsh Guards' column. There was Rex perched on his amazing tank, 'Orpheus', which he had painted all over with nymphs and shepherdesses and harps and gods and cherubs and heaven knows what else. He was drinking coffee in the sun and watching the vast air armada droning overhead, blackening the sky. It was a colossal combined British and American bomber force, which was to pulverize every town and village in Normandy that lay in the path of our projected armoured thrust. When the air assault was over, the GAD was to move into the attack with two other armoured divisions. We were all anxious, butterflies in our tummies, dry in the mouth, trying to make jokes. Some members of the two other divisions had been in battle before in the Middle East, but for us, it was our 'opening night' and the curtain was about to rise. The battle began and was bloody and disastrous. As we rolled forward across the flat dusty country past the Carpiquet airfield, past flattened villages called Benoville, Escoville and such, I saw tank after tank blow up, burst into flames

. . . one quite close to me that got hit by a German 88mm gun early on was commanded by Sir Arthur Grant of our 2nd Bn. and he was killed. The grim day ended with the armoured thrust halted at Cagny; we dug in, the Germans shelled and mortared our positions, the rain fell; we crouched in our slit trenches in the root fields and among the shattered villages. Casualty reports began to come in. We'd lost some officers and quite a lot of men. Then someone from 5th Guards Brigade HQ, a liaison officer of sorts, who was conveying a message to our adjutant, remarked in my hearing, quite casually: 'The Welsh Guards lost some people . . . Rex Whistler was killed . . . rotten luck . . . got out of his tank and ran across to speak to his troop sergeant because his radio was out of action . . . silly thing to do . . . a mortar bomb got him.'

I was depressed, wet and scared enough as it was that evening. But that piece of news coming at the end of a grim and frightening day, as we lay in terror in our little wet holes in the ground, darkened my horizon and made my heart ache, for all of us, for Caroline Paget, for his brother Laurence, for Edith Olivier, for all those many people who loved and admired him. He was someone very, very special and he was dead. I thought of all the romantic young poets who had died in Flanders, including my nephew's namesake and forebear, Julian Grenfell and his brother. Of Byron. Of Rupert Brooke, who succumbed to septicaemia in Salonika. The tragic waste of a young artist, who could give such beauty to the world, dying on a dusty battlefield. And there Rex had been a few hours earlier that morning sitting on his painted tank, laughing in the sun, loved by his men. His work, bequeathed to all who cherish beauty, style and elegance, will ensure his immortality.

— TEN —

I Become an Impresario Once More

When the cease-fire sounded in Western Europe in May 1945 and what Field-Marshal Montgomery called 'the German War' ended, our mob, the 1st Bn. Grenadier Guards, found itself near a small town called Stade close to Verden on the Aller River in Hanover. With intense relief, we set about making ourselves as comfortable as possible for a week or two, until the authorities decided upon our final area of occupation.

Those first few weeks were something of a muddled dream, a kind of blur. The weather was grilling hot, we were tired and dirty and unable to get used to the peace after the thundering of guns and the shell fire. I was billeted in a charming, cool, clean white stucco house in Stade with the local *Zahnarzt* whose tall and rather gorgeous daughter acted as her father's dental nurse in the surgery; she was called Anna and I met her one night, quite late, in the kitchen in her dressing gown and on an impulse kissed her. This was my first and most exciting act of fraternization with the German people, which was at that time strictly forbidden. Anna was enchanting and on two later occasions she accompanied me to a large but deserted church in Stade where of an afternoon, I used to climb up to the organ loft and play not Bach fugues but the only kind of music I can play, which was at that time stuff like the Warsaw Concerto, 'Smoke Gets In Your Eyes' and Hoagy Carmichael. It was a strange feeling, only days after the war had ended, to be seated in the organ loft of a German church in the heart of Hanover, playing a Rita Hayworth number with a tall, cool German blonde on the seat beside me.

We got in a lot of swimming that fortnight too and when May ended and it was June, the Battalion staged in a meadow a 'Fourth of June' celebration day with a cricket match and a 'Procession of Boats' represented by a number of officers 'rowing' across a field in upturned school benches with pennants flying from them. A Latin telegram was sent to the Provost of Eton and much captured wine was consumed.

At the end of June the Guards Armoured Division was sent down to its final occupation area on the Rhine with HQ at Bad Godesberg, near Bonn. As soon as we arrived in the new area and recovered from the shock of seeing Cologne laid waste by bombing, the Battalion was ordered to Berlin to find a guard of honour for the Allied victory parades there. At the same time, as a result of the many improvised concerts and shows I had written and staged along the way through France, Belgium and Holland, I was appointed to work under my dear old friend Nico Llewellyn-Davies, Deputy Assistant Director of Army Welfare Services (DADAWS) to the Guards Armoured Division, as Entertainments Officer with the rank of temporary major and I was directed to take up residence at B Mess, Divisional HQ at Bad Godesberg.

This new appointment prevented me from going with my old shower to Berlin, where I missed witnessing a surprising event. Timothy Tufnell was conducting Marshal Zhukov on a tour of inspection down the ranks of his company, which was finding the guard of honour for the Soviet VIPs, when he was frankly goosed from the rear by Marshal Rokkososvsky. The Soviet war leader, it seems, prodded Timothy's bottom with his sword in an attempt to slow down the pace, thus enabling the lesser generals behind to catch up.

My old half-track, named 'Swanage', all spit and polish as be-fitted the technical adjutant's personal vehicle, had the honour of carrying Churchill, Eden, Eisenhower, Monty and General Marshall in the Victory Parade; this completely turned its head.

Life during the year from June 1945 to February 1946, when I was demobilized and returned to the UK, was one of the most interesting, exciting and disturbing periods of my life. I had an office, a staff, including two German secretaries and Frank Curzon, a charming subaltern in the Scots Guards, exclusive use of a jeep and driver and I was responsible for providing entertainment for all British and Allied Troops in an area the size of Wales.

Of this entertainment, in the first months after the war, only very little was provided by ENSA. There were, it's true, various itinerant little parties of third-rate music-hall performers travelling round the Rhine Army Zone, as they had during the battle period; singing, dancing and jokes were provided by accordionplaying blondes of uncertain age and rather tired stand-up comics. There began to appear too, in the major cities, such as Brussels and Hamburg, rather smart H. M. Tennent productions of West End plays with stars in the John Gielgud, Vivien Leigh bracket. My 'command' and responsibility, however, was all the native German talent that lay bruised and battered under our feet. In my area were the skeletons of three civic symphony orchestras and opera companies, each with its own ballet – those of Cologne, Aachen and Bonn. There were also, potentially, dozens of singers, pianists, violinists, cellists and other musicians of international repute, whose homes were or had been in and around our devastated cities.   I requested and received *carte blanche* from my superiors to resuscitate all this musical talent from the rubble and to get some opera, concerts and ballet going for the pleasure and enlightenment of our troops and for the morale of the dazed and shocked German civil population. Money being of no possible use in those early days before the new Occupation marks came into being, the currency was food, shelter, cigarettes and above all, encouragement.

I have never ceased to bless the day I became a modern languages specialist at Eton and went on through travel abroad to become fluent in French and German. I could speak to the Germans and I could speak to them about music.

Day after day, I would set out in my jeep to drive to some remote village down the Rhine, where I had perhaps been told there lived a great bass, who had sung Sarastro in *Zauberflöte* in the Cologne Opera for years. I would arrive at a villa to find a sad, lined woman living alone. 'Herr Gröschel is at the war, on the Eastern Front. I have not heard from him for a year. I fear he is dead or at best *Kriegsgefangener.*' So I would leave. 'Let me know if you hear news.'

Perhaps a week later at the Bonn Railway Station a battered, shell-torn wreck of a train would pull in, its windows broken, its carriages crammed with ill and wounded German prisoners-of-war, repatriated from Russia. The liaison officer of the Red Cross would check the roll for me. 'No Gröschel but there is a Corporal Klaus Hafner.' I check my list. Hafner is the flautist we need to complete the woodwind section of the Cologne Opera Orchestra. They'd given him up for dead. He is seized, taken home, bathed, fed; we find his flute in a cupboard in his house. His wife is weeping with joy. Tonight, Klaus will play for a performance of *Don Giovanni* in Krefeld. But Klaus says he is weak after months of hell in a Russian camp. He needs rehearsal. But he makes it and his life is restored. I know I am very sentimental and emotional and too easily moved by too much. I also love music as much as life itself. I make no bones about it: to find myself in a position to organize performances of opera, symphony concerts and ballet evenings, to arrange, say, an all-out *Fidelio* in the Bonn University Hall with improvised scenery and costumes; to see the whole German cast and orchestra lining up before the performance for a bowl of soup and a packet of fags as their renumeration; then their tired, worn faces light up with new hope as they tune their instruments and return to normal life (of a kind); and perhaps most of all, to hear the deep-throated roars of applause and the standing ovations given by halls full of Guardsmen and Gunners – many of whom had never been near an opera house or a symphony concert in their lives – to the musicians, singers and dancers of their defeated enemies; it all affected me very deeply. I began to realize how those little black and white dots on a stave were, apart from the morse code, the only totally international language, a means of communication and understanding between peoples of different race and tongue.

It used to strike me very much, the thought that you could assemble sixty or seventy Germans of all ages, men, women and youths, some almost in rags, all hungry, defeated, broken, mourning their dead, afraid for the future, and sit them at orchestral desks with the correct band parts before them for, let us say the Beethoven 4th in B flat major. Another German comes to the rostrum, equally sad, broken and hungry but with enough strength to lift his baton. In a flash, the air is filled with the most glorious, ethereal God-given sound. But, give or take a minor detail of speed or balance, it is the same sound that may be emanating at that same moment from the well-dressed, well-fed, well-paid London Symphony Orchestra in the Albert Hall in the heart of London, playing as the buses rumble past outside. And it is the same sound again that may be echoing round the ample ceiling of a great stone concert hall in Moscow or Philadelphia. Other men and women with other problems are scraping, bowing and blowing away, flipping over the pages at their music desks, and somehow the whole world is playing Beethoven, everywhere, and it is as though all those countries thousands of miles apart in distance, in political system and in culture are speaking to each other with one voice.

One performance I managed to organize with the great assistance of my German music contact, an elderly professor called Julius Gless, who lived in Godesberg and had long retired as Intendant of the Cologne Opera, was the First Act of *Die Walküre*.

Owing to the late unlamented Fuhrer's affection for Wagner, it had been decreed somewhere, probably at SHAEF HQ that Wagner's music was not to be played or sung anywhere in defeated Germany. Unaware of this ruling, Gless and I scraped together an orchestra, induced a local carpenter to run up a sort of Hunding's hut and a forest backing, cut up some army blankets from our QM stores for costumes and contacted a tenor, just back from the front, who knew the role of Sigmund. Gless knew of a middle-aged soprano in Konigswinter across the river, who had sung Sieglinde many times in her youth. She was American by birth but had lived for years in Germany as the wife of a German university professor at Bonn. It remained to find a Hunding. After a day or two of fruitless searching, Gless, himself a former operatic bass, offered his services. Of course, he'd known all along that there were no basses in the area and it was he who had suggested doing *Die Walküre*. I discovered later that his Hunding had been famous all over South Germany. It was a charming, if devious, way of getting himself on stage again before he was too old.

We gave the *Valkyrie* First Act in a park theatre in Godesberg with the audience sitting in the open under the moon. It was very affecting. It was also, I believe (and I'm ready to be challenged on this) the very first performance of Wagner to take place in Germany after the Second World War.

In 1946 I returned from Germany to London, reported to the demob. barracks in Albany Street, Regent's Park, received a free suit of clothes, overcoat and soft hat and rejoined millions of my contemporaries in 'civvy street'. I was thirty.

ACT TWO

Old Brandy

— ELEVEN —

I Get a Break with Balcon

Most careers have turning points and they are usually people. The successful musician will describe how the great conductor once heard him play at some obscure charity concert and asked him to join his orchestra; a schoolmaster with a passion for drama will unwittingly start a boy on an acting career by communicating that passion during rehearsals for the school play; a single paragraph of praise from a respected critic will determine a wavering Sunday novelist to give up his job at the town hall and write full-time.

When I was demobilized from the army in 1946 and found myself unemployed and virtually penniless, Sir Michael Balcon gave me a job in his film studios at Ealing and at the age of thirty my second – or postwar – career began. He was a turning point in my life.

I'm a bit ashamed to reveal how I got that job at Ealing Studios but I will be honest. All I knew in that confused year was that I wanted to get back into some area of show business. I believed myself to be talented in various directions: as a revue lyric writer, song writer, sketch writer and short story writer and I had a first stage play tucked away in my drawer at home. So I sat down and wrote letters to just about every individual and organization in show business I could think of, including the BBC. I was ready to do anything for a start – sweep the stage or the studio floor, make the tea, type, run errands. . . . I even wrote to some of the larger agencies such as Myron Selznick, Linnit and Dunfee, and Gordon Harbord. And I wrote to the Windmill Theatre.

All these letters were penned without a single qualm of conscience on Windsor Castle notepaper, for the perfectly valid reason that I was living there at the time. My mother and stepfather having been bombed out of their 'grace and favour' house at St James's Palace in 1944, had been offered by Their Majesties a small but charming residence in the left-hand tower of the Henry VIII Gateway of Windsor Castle. As an unmarried, out-of-work ex-officer I saw no reason to live elsewhere. It was comfortable and it was free.

The replies to my letters were discouraging, until one morning an Ealing Studios envelope came with a letter from Mr Balcon in person. 'Always anxious to help ex-service people . . . make an appointment with my secretary . . . see what can be done. . . .' It was the first and, but for an offer from the BBC to interview me for a training course for Light Entertainment assistant producers, the only positive result.

I blessed Mick Balcon that day without having met him, though as a student of the cinema his name was well known to me. The following morning I went down in the Tube to Ealing Studios and, as I passed through the modest gate and headed for his office in a sort of lodge with a lawn, rose-garden and cedar tree, I remembered visiting the same studios in 1937 to lunch with Frances Day, who was making *The Girl in the Taxi* with an up-and-coming young director called Carol Reed. Balcon asked me why on earth I wanted to enter the film business. I told him I'd written some revue material, had two magazine stories published and saw myself as a writer-director. So he sent for Stella Jonckheere, a brilliantly clever lady who ran the literary department of the scenario dept. Her job was to look out for properties – new novels, plays and original film stories – to deal in rights and options, and to furnish readers' reports on possible material for the resident producers. It was agreed that I should be taken on as an 'inside reader'. Material sent in to the scenario department at the studios was normally farmed out to a network of erudite but impoverished spinsters and widows, who for a fee of ten shillings to a guinea, would read the MS or proof copy of a new novel or stage play and type out a synopsis of the plot with details of author, agent, etc., and an opinion on its suitability as film material. These were the 'outside readers' and I was to be one of a small group who did just that inside the studios. So Michael Balcon hired me for a modest salary and from 4 April, 1946, I was in films.

I had realized one of my principal daydreams, for a career in films had been in my mind ever since a winter afternoon in 1930 when my brother and I and some cousins were invited down to the British International Pictures studios at Elstree to watch a film being made. There was a wonderful character there called Joe Grossman, the studio manager, a cockney Jewish wag, known and loved by nearly everybody in films – for Elstree was then the centre of British films and BIP the major studio. My stepfather had met Joe somewhere, who had said to him: 'Bring the family down, Major, any time you like.' So we arrived, a party of wide-eyed schoolboys, and were duly ushered on to the set.

As I recall there were two talking films in production that day at BIP. One was called *Fascination* and a scene from it was being filmed with Kay Hammond, then a young dizzy blonde wearing a very low-cut satin dress, and a funny man called Kenneth Cove, who played what were known as 'dude' parts. The director was the actor, Miles Mander.

For two hours we stood discreetly in the shadows and watched these two players go through a comedy seduction scene. No one, watching film-making for the first time, can ever quite get over the seemingly endless 'takes'. To the layman film-making seems a painfully slow, time-wasting business. 'My dear, they went over the scene twenty times – exactly the same.' Of course it wasn't the same. There was a slight dialogue fluff on Take 1. A microphone shadow across the star's bosom on Take 2. A door stuck on Take 3. The actor got his line back to front on Take 4. The operator lost the actor's head, as he rose from his chair in Take 5. Sound couldn't hear the star's last line clearly on Take 6. And so on through the afternoon. At all events, watching two players go up to Take 11 that afternoon in 1930 did not bore me for one moment. I was fascinated by *Fascination* and something inside me said that one day I must direct a film. From that day on films were in my blood.

Soon after that visit to Elstree I was taken to Gaumont-British at Lime Grove where Hitchcock was at work on an early master-piece, and later on my old school friend David Parsons, son of Viola Tree and Alan Parsons, occasionally asked me down to lunch at Denham Studios, where he was acting in Korda pictures under contract as David Tree.

London Films at Denham was the nearest we ever got to real 'Hollywood' glamour in British films in the 'thirties. Korda filled those studios with international stars, directors, cameramen, writers and designers and created his own special charismatic atmosphere. David Tree was in *Knight without Armour* and through him I watched Marlene Dietrich and Robert Donat scrambling through a thick Russian forest built on one of the stages; I also spotted Robert Taylor eating a salad in the studio restaurant at a time when he was the world's most expensive heart-throb.

On another occasion, visiting Denham with Tony Pelissier to watch Johnny Mills working on a picture, I met and lunched with Laurence Olivier, who was playing in *The Divorce of Lady X* with Merle Oberon by day and *Hamlet* at the Old Vic by night. For some reason I remember he had metal taps on his black patent leather evening shoes, such as hoofers wear. When someone pointed this out, he replied: 'Yes, *"Hamlet* in Taps" ' and giggled engagingly.

Now in 1946 I was actually employed in films myself and with the famous Michael Balcon. As I progressed from inside reader to personal assistant on various films and assisted at the birth of so many of the now famous Ealing comedies on the studio floor, in the cutting rooms and in the dubbing theatre, I saw more and more of Balcon and became a friend of his family. I was invited to stay for weekends at Upper Parrock, his beautiful old Sussex farm-house, where I met his wife, Aileen, his talented and velvet-voiced daughter, Jill, and his son, Jonathan. The Balcons were and are a warm, loving and close-knit family.

When Jill married Cecil Day Lewis, who had taught me Latin at Summer Fields, I was delighted, for I was extremely fond of her and knew how she adored him. Mick had reservations about the liaison at first, mainly, I suspect, because, with his very orthodox views on marriage, he did not relish the prospects of his only daughter marrying a divorced man some years her senior. I once mentioned to him that one day he might find himself the father-in-law of the Poet Laureate. Mick grunted. It was meant as a joke. In the end, of course, Mick came to accept Jill's happy and blessed marriage with pride and joy.

I do not think films were ever far from Mick Balcon's mind. He was, of course, a man with an enormous variety of interests: a patron of art, music, ballet and opera, politically committed, a keen cricketer and a great lover of the live theatre. But films dominated his life.

One weekend at Upper Parrock, he took me tramping across the wet fields to visit his farm and check the milk-yield figures of his cows, which he scanned with the same intensity as he would the box-office receipts of one of his pictures. We'd been talking about cattle and there was a long silence as we trudged on, the wind blowing our macs, the rain beating down. Mick was deep in thought. About his farm problems, I imagined. Suddenly he stopped dead in his tracks and said: 'Thorold Dickinson wants to make *The Mayor of Casterbridge* you know. But the rights aren't free.' Then he walked on towards the cowsheds. Perhaps the country setting had reminded him of Hardy.

Monja Danischewsky, who handled the publicity for the studios before becoming a producer and screenwriter, told a nice story about Balcon, who always arrived at and left the studio in his chauffeur-driven car. One day, Aileen kept the car in London for shopping rather later than usual and Mick wanted to leave the studio early. So 'Danny', who was with Mick at the time, said: 'You'll have to come up with me on the Tube', and led his chief along the road to South Ealing Underground Station. As they rattled along through Acton, Hammersmith and Earl's Court Mick, in his black Homburg and clutching his umbrella, showed the wide-eyed excitement and fascination of a child on its first trip in a train. According to Danny he bounced up and down on his seat exclaiming, 'You know, these seats are really damn comfortable.' Then the train stopped at their station. 'Danny,' he said as they got out at Knightsbridge, 'that was most interesting. We must make a film about the Tube. Most interesting.'

One night during my first few weeks as a reader in the scenario department at Ealing, I was dancing at a private party with Princess Elizabeth, whom I had met on and off at Windsor Castle parties and who had often visited our Grenadier Guards Battalion as Colonel of the Regiment. As we danced, she asked me what I was doing now, so I told her I was working in a film studio out at Ealing. She seemed highly intrigued and asked if she might come down and visit the studios one day. I said I was sure it could be arranged.

Next day I asked to see Mick and told him of the Princess's request. The effect was electrifying. Mick rang bells and picked up telephones. A date was arranged and later Joey told me that he would be coming down himself with the *two* Princesses – for

Princess Margaret had asked to come as well.

When they arrived at the studios, Miss Crawford, the royal governess, was also in the party. We were making *Nicholas Nickleby* at the time, so the Princesses met Cedric Hardwicke, Derek Bond, Mary Merrall and Sally Ann Howes, not to mention the director, Cavalcanti.

One feature of that informal royal visit to Ealing Studios was Mick's concern that on the day chosen by Buck House for the visit, he had invited the Hollywood columnist Hedda Hopper to lunch and could not reach her to postpone. So Hedda came down too in one of her extraordinary hats and spent a whole day going round the studios with the Princesses, achieving a pretty good scoop for herself in the *Hollywood Reporter*. But Mick handled it all with superb diplomacy and that nervous charm that endeared him to all.

One summer night in 1949, less than a year after the Princesses' visit to Ealing Studios, the Duke of Wellington lent Apsley House to Lady Serena James to give a dance for her daughter Ursula. At some point during the evening I asked Princess Elizabeth for the honour of a dance. She was inevitably very booked up but promised me in her charming, impeccably polite way 'the next but two'. I thanked her and we agreed to meet on the landing outside the ballroom underneath an oil painting of a white horse, which was exactly where we were standing at the time. I went off to the bar and, after a couple of dances, arrived back at the rendezvous to find no sign of my partner to be. Someone told me that she had left a few minutes earlier and that part of the reason was that news had leaked in Fleet Street that evening of her engagement to Prince Philip, although it was not supposed to be announced officially from the Palace until the next day. The result of the 'leak' was that vast crowds had gathered outside Apsley House to see the Princess leave the ball.

At any rate, I duly wrote to congratulate her on her engagement and she replied with a typically thoughtful and amusing letter which I shall treasure always and pass on in a tin box to my heirs and successors. In it she apologized for missing our dance, explaining that she had decided to go home early and had looked for me to explain. She must have been tired after a hectic and exciting day.

News of her engagement reminded me of a smaller, less formal party given for the two Princesses by Princess Marina, the Duchess

of Kent, at Coppins just after I had returned from Germany in
1946. On that occasion I played the piano as usual and remember
noticing how particularly happy and bright H.R.H. seemed that
evening as she leant over the piano and asked me to play Cole
Porter's 'When They Begin the Beguine'. Out of the corner of my
eye I saw a very handsome young naval officer chatting away by
the window. Later someone said he was Prince Philip of Greece
and that H.R.H. was rather 'taken with him'.

I remember little else about that party except that we had to play
'The Game', at which, of course, Princess Margaret excelled, for
she was and is so witty and such a clever mimic that she could have
earned her living on the stage at any time.

The King and Queen were always interested to meet celebrities
of the stage and screen and Joey was aware of this. At Windsor one
Sunday soon after the war, when the King and Queen came to
drinks before lunch at our curious little round tower in the Henry
VIII Gateway, I suggested asking David and Prim Niven, as they
were then living in the little village of Dorney beyond Eton.

Poor Prim was great with child and had to sit down all the time
in the window-seat while the King talked to her. David, of course,
amused Queen Elizabeth enormously. It was the last time I saw
Prim Niven before her tragic death in Hollywood.

On another occasion, in 1947, when the King and Queen came
to evening drinks with us at St James's, Mama and Joey invited
Ruth Draper, the famous American 'diseuse', for them to meet. As
a great friend of Lady Astor's sister Mrs Phipps, the mother of
Joyce Grenfell, I always suspected that Ruth Draper had been the
chief inspiration to the equally brilliant Mrs Grenfell.

On that same evening Tom Arnold, the impresario, whom Joey
knew well, and Mick and Aileen Balcon also came. It was only a
matter of days later that Mick received his knighthood. Perhaps
Joey knew and wanted His Majesty to meet informally at least one
of his new Knights Bachelor.

It was affectionately said of Mick by many who worked with
him that he was sometimes guilty of over-caution, which prevented
him from becoming the legendary, wildly extravagant film-
impresario figure of a Korda or a del Guidice, and just as well. An
example of this caution is illustrated by a letter he once wrote to
Harry Watt, who was having some trouble with the Australian
authorities over a location. Mick's letter to Harry ended with the

words: 'Rest assured, my dear Harry, that I will back you up to the hilt.' But after some reflection Mick amended it. The final version ended: 'I will back you up.'

To this day I am proud to have been given my first break in films and later to have been promoted to the rank of producer by the man who discovered Hitchcock and probably did more for British films than anyone in history. Michael Balcon was a wonderful boss and a major influence in my career. I shall always be grateful to him.

The real 'Ealing comedy' period began on the very first day that I took up my duties in the scenario department. This does not mean that I, personally, gave the order for the comedies to begin filming. It just happened that my first day at the studios was the first day of studio shooting on *Hue and Cry* with Alastair Sim and others, written by the prolific T. E. B. Clarke, directed by Charles Crichton and produced by Henry Cornelius.

It was in 'Corney's' office that a corner had been found for me to sit, while I waded through Victor Hugo's vast novel *Toilers of the Sea* trying to grasp the plot and characters in order to compose my first 'subject report' as to whether I considered it possible film material. I did and said so but it was never made.

However, Corney rather took me over and I went with him down to the set to watch the filming of *Hue and Cry,* glad of the relief from Victor Hugo. In due course I became personal assistant to Cornelius and worked closely with him on two of his subsequent pictures, *It Always Rains on Sunday* and *Passport to Pimlico.* I began to learn how films were made. I worked in the cutting rooms and on the floor as an assistant; I attended music-recording sessions, dubbing sessions and of course, endless script and story conferences.

These latter ceremonies took place in the office of Angus McPhail, the studio script editor, a brilliant story consultant and manipulator-stimulator of writers, whose advice, skill and above all, diplomacy as a chairman, saved many a story conference from breaking up in confusion with fisticuffs between irate writers and a stubborn director or producer. For films at Ealing were planned most carefully at the story outline stage and on into the script stage more or less in committee.

After 'Tibby' Clarke had conceived his brilliant idea for *Passport to Pimlico* a whole string of story conferences were held in

McPhail's office to thrash out the storyline, before Tibby started to script it. Day after day we sat in a circle, Cornelius, Tibby Clarke, Angus, Ted (E.V.H.) Emmett, the famous Gaumont-British news-caster, who was to produce, and I, in my capacity of personal assistant to the director, Henry Cornelius.

The central situation of the film was mad enough – a street corner in Pimlico proving through the discovery of ancient docu-ments buried deep in the earth below to have been ceded in medieval times to Burgundy and thus to be no longer a part of Great Britain. This uproariously funny premise was so loaded with comic possibilities that we all lost our heads and there was a danger of the picture lapsing into slapstick farce. I remember one day we were discussing the famous 'siege sequence', when the people of 'Little Burgundy' were holding out against H.M. Government and asserting their independence, and the outside world was trying to get food through to the London Burgundians; we were all suggest-ing fantastic ideas such as a helicopter delivering the milk and buns being thrown down from a passing train. . . . In the end these two ideas were used but one suggestion from Tibby Clark that was not used was the idea of a group of Chelsea Pensioners in the Royal Hospital not so far away secretly making puddings and firing them out of the ancient cannons down into the little beleaguered area of South London.

One of my tasks later on, when the film was being shot on the bomb-site location just over Lambeth Bridge and under the rail-way viaduct, was to accompany a crowd of some fifty film extras backwards and forwards by every train that ran from Waterloo to Vauxhall all of one day, giving them the cue through a mega-phone to hurl their bags of buns out of the train windows, as we passed over the location and the waiting camera.

One small contribution I was able to make towards the film, apart from some three lines in the dialogue, was the wording of the various newspaper headlines seen in the film, commenting on the 'political situation' of Little Burgundy. In a montage of news-papers are *The Times* headline: 'Territorial Anomaly Solved in South London' and that of the *Daily Mirror*: 'Women Weep as "Burgundy" Totters'. I was rather pleased with that.

Another vintage Ealing comedy on which I worked in a minor capacity was the rather off-beat but highly praised Edwardian black comedy, *Kind Hearts and Coronets*. This film is among the most popular ever produced at Ealing, and there is an interesting story behind the discovery of its subject.

A staff writer in the studios, Michael Pertwee, was spending a weekend in the dormy house of a south coast golf club, where his sparse bedroom bookshelf boasted not only the Holy Bible, the *Bradshaw* of 1913 and *Ruff's Guide to the Turf,* inscribed with the words 'Not To Be Taken Away', but a musty, tattered Edwardian novel in a red cover, bearing advertisements for Pear's Soap and Camp Coffee. It was called *Israel Rank* by Roy Horniman. Mike Pertwee, preferring the novel to the other offerings, started to read it in bed. By three o'clock in the morning he was laughing out loud. It told in the first person the story of Israel Rank, the Jewish and illegitimate member of a great English ducal family, who needed to murder a number of his relations in order to suceed to the dukedom.

This he did but he was finally caught and went to the gallows. What struck Mike Pertwee was not so much the black comedy element of an elegant and gracious novel about murder but the incredibly witty, Oscar Wildean style of the central character's first person comments and observations. Mike somehow 'obtained' the precious book from the golf club – I believe it was the only copy we ever had – and everyone concerned read it. Mike wrote a treatment of it.

I saw at once a faint resemblance in flavour to Oscar Wilde's *Lord Arthur Savile's Crime.* The novel also had affinities with a very funny French film I had recently seen, Sacha Guitry's *Roman d'un Tricheur.* Another black comedy, it concerned a poisoning achieved with mushrooms. Here again we had the witty, first-person commentary running offscreen in deliciously ironical contrast or relation to the events we saw on the screen. This was clearly the right style for a film of *Israel Rank.* I said so and was promptly ordered to get on to the Film Archive of the British Film Institute and ask for a copy of the Guitry picture. Originally *Kind Hearts* was to extend the happy partnership of *It Always Rains on Sunday* with the talented Robert Hamer directing and Cornelius producing. But Corney had tasted blood with *Pimlico* and was now only interested in direction. So Michael Relph, son of the famous Old Vic actor, George Relph, and a very gifted set and costume designer, turned producer, joined forces with Hamer and the project was scheduled.

There was a tendency at Ealing in those days, as in other studios, to find a subject then hire the most expensive and reputable writer that money could buy to do the script. It was a Hollywood habit that has never really died in films and reflects a nervousness on the part of film producers. If something goes wrong with the picture and you can turn round and say, 'After all the script was by Harold Pinter (or Terence Rattigan or Graham Greene),' it somehow manages to excuse the producer's failure and enables him to live to fight another day. It's a form of insurance, like the star system. If you have Paul Newman and Dustin Hoffman in a bad film you can blame its failure on them, for not 'pulling them in'.

When possible writers for *'Israel Rank'* were discussed, Hamer suggested Evelyn Waugh. So Evelyn Waugh's agents were contacted and the novelist agreed to come down to the studios for lunch and, without commitment, discuss the book and the project generally. By this time I had obtained a very scratched old copy of Sacha Guitry's *Roman d'un Tricheur* and it was resolved to run this picture for Evelyn Waugh and suggest that his screenplay should follow the Guitry format and style.

I was invited to the lunch because I had met Waugh at Plas Newydd a year or so previously. The lunch went off quite well, as did the running of Guitry's film. Eventually Waugh left, saying he would think about it. A matter of hours later, his agent telephoned to say that after careful consideration of the kind offer, Mr Waugh would prefer not to write a film script based on another novelist's work. Roy Horniman, in fact, had been dead and buried some twenty-five years, but one could see his point.

In the end an extremely able studio staff-writer, John Dighton, took it on and worked closely with Robert Hamer to produce an excellent script, in which Israel Rank, for reasons of Semitic sensibility, became an Italian. The title was changed to *Kind Hearts and Coronets.*

My principal contribution to that picture was the acquisition of two major locations. The first was Leeds Castle near Maidstone, where as I have related I used to stay quite often as a guest of its owner, the wealthy Lady Baillie, sister of racehorse-owner Dorothy Paget; this moated, expensively restored medieval castle seemed to the producers an ideal location for the D'Ascoyne family's country seat. It was no problem to persuade Olive Baillie to allow filming there, since her husband, Sir Adrian Baillie, had been an MP with a special interest in the film industry, and her weekend guests at Leeds often included movie stars. David Niven, Ray Milland, Douglas Fairbanks and many others are to be found in the Visitors' Book there.

Another film star in Olive's circle of friends was Valerie Hobson, then married to Anthony Havelock-Allan. She played a leading role in *Kind Hearts* and, when the unit went down to film at Leeds, Olive invited her and Dennis Price to stay in the castle. Alec Guinness was invited too but wisely declined, fearing social activity in the evening might distract him from the enormous concentration he needed for his now world-famous portrayal of the various D'Ascoyne relations, including the aunt.

There was also a boating sequence in *Kind Hearts,* in which, after scenes on the lawn of a smart riverside hotel, akin to Skindles, one of the younger D'Ascoyne female cousins played by a lovely young blonde actress, now the talented writer Anne Valery, was allowed to slide over the weir in a punt after a day on the river with Louis. The latter, it will be recalled, reflected to himself that 'after all the young lady was spared from suffering a fate worse than death'. This amusing scene was duly filmed at the Guards Boat Club, Maidenhead, which is, alas, no more. At the time I was a member thereof and to obtain permission for filming there, I had to meet the Committee of the Guards Boat Club in a room at the Guards Club in London. As a former Grenadier officer, I felt fairly confident of success, especially as Ealing Studios offered to pay a sum of money into the club funds. But other considerations worried the small group of senior Guards officers seated round the table. I had told them breezily that we wanted to film scenes wherein 'a number of young bloods and some actresses from the theatre would be disporting themselves on a lawn beside the Thames, drinking and flirting'.

From the glum expression on their faces, you would have thought they envisaged a number of half-naked chorus girls rolling about on the grass with their boyfriends. I discovered later that that was precisely what they *had* envisaged. I had omitted the pertinent fact that the scene was set in 1903 and the actresses would be dressed in long, lace and ribboned dresses, picture hats and carrying parasols, with their swains in blazers and straw-boaters.

This final reassurance and a sizeable cheque opened the doors to us and a very happy day's filming took place on the lawns of the old Guards Boat Club.

Not long before shooting began on *Kind Hearts* the press show was announced of Chaplin's new film, *Monsieur Verdoux*. It was soon learned that this too was to be a comedy about a mass murderer, set in late Victorian times. Chaplin, of course, had Landru in mind, the Paris Bluebeard of the 'nineties. On press show day we all went to the New Gallery cinema in some trepidation to see how far we were encroaching on Chaplin's territory. Or rather he on ours. We were, to a great extent; or rather he was. But we told ourselves that *Kind Hearts* was a more literate piece, depending on witty dialogue and elegant playing scenes, while Chaplin's film was more visual, relying as he usually did on brilliant mime and business. Also, his story had nothing to do with a man killing relations in order to inherit a dukedom.

Oddly enough, no comparisons were ever drawn between the two films, even though both pictures contained one identical visual joke. Chaplin had done in one of his victims and was burning the body in an incinerator, from which tell-tale smoke was seen darkening the sky in the distance as he spoke to someone in the foreground. In *Kind Hearts* Louis had blown up a cousin in his photographic dark-room and again smoke was seen darkening the sky over Louis's shoulder as he sat in the garden with his lady love. I suppose it was coincidence.

Ealing Studios was literally a film school for young technicians and writers, with Mick Balcon as the headmaster. A number of excellent actors and actresses appeared in several Ealing films and these players became the nearest thing ever seen to a film repertory company: Alec Guinness, Googie Withers, Jack Warner, Mervyn Johns, Gordon Jackson, John Slater, Donald Houston, John Gregson, Joan Greenwood, to name a few. There was a marvellous team spirit at Ealing and everyone on the lot had a sense of belonging.

What was so wonderful and alas exists no longer with the closure of the major film studios and the coming of independent production, was the continuing flow of output. As one film started shooting at Ealing, the one before was in the cutting rooms and the next one was in the script stage or on location. Only TV companies can work like that today and provide permanent employment for all.

The contract directors and producers knew their plans for years

ahead and could spend studio money finding and developing
subjects with the certainty that there would be funds with which
to make them, provided Balcon agreed. Some people say that this
method resulted in a stereotyped product, all the films coming out
with the same kind of stamp or style and nothing in them that was
very startling, original or daring. This may be true. But it should
also be said that Ealing films never fell below a fairly high level of
quality in writing, acting and direction. And they were made with
a great emphasis on the love of the job, rather than a desire to
make a quick buck. This was probably the secret of Ealing's
success.

— TWELVE —

I Married an Angel

It was while I was working at Ealing Studios that I encountered
Jean, my first and only wife and the mother of my two sons. I
have long had a theory that there comes in a young man's life a
psychological moment, a point in his development, even a change
in his attitude, when he suddenly feels 'It's time I got married'; at
this point he goes out and gets married to whichever girl he is
currently going around with. This may be a monstrous over-
simplification but I do believe there is something in it. A young
man may decide to marry when he gets his inheritance from a dead
father, or when his mother dies, or when he lands a good job, or
possibly when his closest friends marry.

What I am trying to say is I do not really believe that men con-
sciously move through life searching for the ideal girl, find her and
at that moment, whatever the situation, marry.

A friend of mine, when war broke out in 1939, told me he
thought he ought to have a wife if he was going off to the war. He
said he should have someone to worry about him (imagine the self-
ishness!) and promptly went out the same evening and proposed
to the girl he happened quite by chance to be sitting with in a nightclub. He had dozens of girls to choose from, but he evidently felt:
'I've got to get married quick. I'm with Sarah tonight. I quite like
her. She'll do.' And that was that. They are to this very day together, happy and contented.

By the time I was demobilized from the Rhine Army of Occupation in 1946, I was thirty. I had carefully avoided marrying at
the outbreak of or during the war. Now I was getting on, I'd seen
life and was living in great comfort once again at St James's Palace,
waited on by servants, and just beginning my new post-war career

105

in the scenario department at Ealing Studios. It was my moment to stop being a bachelor and share my life with someone.

A brother Grenadier and close friend, Timothy Tufnell, rang me up one day about this time and told me that he and his mother, the famous Mrs N. C. Tufnell, Great Britain's first and best lady house-agent, were planning to present a revue in the village hall at Sunninghill to raise funds for the Waifs and Strays. Would I care to assist?

Timothy and I had laughed and camped our way through the war together. He was immensely brave and had won a very good MC in Germany. When he wasn't being brave, Timothy, who travelled with one of his mother's old tea gowns, a wig and some high-heeled shoes in his kit, used to dress up and prance about in the mess after dinner and amuse even the stuffiest of the senior officers.

Timothy's project sounded fun. I agreed and we proceeded to put together an Intimate Revue, using the title and some of my unused material from my ill-fated 1939 project, 'Fiddlesticks'. Some young people, male and female, were recruited to augment the cast; Timothy and his mother, Sybil, were to star. I began to plan the show, nipping down to Fairfield, the Tufnell home at Sunninghill, at weekends to rehearse.

We were, however, short of a girl and George Astley, now Secretary of the Society of Authors, who was around at the time, said he knew of a very attractive girl who was working at the fashion house, Spectator Sports, as secretary to the boss, as well as doing a bit of modelling. George was asked to bring this unknown beauty to Maison Prunier in St James's Street, where he and I would entertain her to dinner and see if she was suitable for our purposes.

I arrived at the restaurant and was confronted with the most shatteringly beautiful, tall, dark and elegant young woman, her hair swept up in the current fashion and wearing what seemed like a disdainful look. I was completely knocked out.

We dined. She said very little but seemed cool and very much at ease. Hardly daring to look at this goddess beside me, I talked incoherently to George about the war, the political situation – anything.

Soon the wine relaxed me and Miss Lodge began to smile too and unbend from what I later realized was not disdain but a charming, natural shyness with strangers.

Needless to say Jean Lodge was talked into appearing in our revue at Sunninghill. Each weekend thereafter I drove her down in my little car to the Tufnells', falling more and more madly in love as we sped down the old Staines road. I favoured her outrageously, gave her much of the best material and spent somewhat more time rehearsing her than the others and she was a hit.

Encouraged by her huge success in *Fiddlesticks* and with a nudge from me, Jean decided to try for a career on the stage. Her parents, elderly and sensible, must have had qualms. But they loved and trusted their daughter, who had been on her own working in London for a year or two and no objection came from her home just outside Hull in Yorkshire.

In due course Jean, by writing dozens of letters, achieved an audition with John Counsell, who smartly engaged her as ASM and to play small parts at the Theatre Royal, Windsor.

She looked even more divine on the stage than off and with her expressive eyes and pleasing voice and above all her grace of deportment and movement acquired from training as a dancer and model, she soon caught the eye of the West End producers. We were married in St James's, Spanish Place on 18 September, 1948. By the time our firstborn child was on the way, Jean had appeared in dozens of films, television plays and repertory productions. Now she was in her first West End part, that of the American daughter-in-law in William Douglas-Home's comedy *The Manor of North-stead*, and pregnant.

Charlie Shaughnessy put an end to that engagement. But later another engagement, that of a nanny, enabled Jean to continue with her career. This was very necessary, as I was still a struggling, underpaid scriptwriter, and we needed money badly.

Jean reached the nearest to what we both wanted for her when she appeared at the Bristol Old Vic in the leading female role of Silia in Pirandello's *The Rules of the Game*. It was a marvellous part and she was stunning. Shortly after that she landed a so-so part in a thriller, *Dead on Nine*, at the Westminster Theatre, but during its run our second child Master David Shaughnessy started making his presence felt and Jean had to leave the cast once more and make for the maternity ward. As the boys grew up, Jean worked less, devoting most and eventually all of her time to them. She was a conscientious and loving mother and her career became secondary.

They did, as a family of three – Mum and the two kids – work for me once or twice for a giggle, appearing in some of my filmed commercials for Eyeline Films and a documentary for the Cable and Wireless Company. They also on one occasion dubbed their voices onto a rather charming little Soviet film called *I Bought a Father* which was released on the Rank Circuit.

Since both our sons were carried pre-natally by their mother on the London stage, it is not surprising that the elder, Charlie, spent much of his time at Cambridge directing productions for the ADC and 'Footlights', while David, the younger, after acting his head off successfully at the Central School of Speech and Drama, is at the time of writing acting in *Hamlet* in Dubrovnik.

Jean and I were conservative to a degree when we named our two sons. We both liked Charles, but I did warn that Charles Shaughnessy was unspeakable, the two s's running awkwardly together and creating a tongue-twister, which as a writer of dialogue for actors to speak, I could not really allow. However, we told ourselves he would become Charlie and he has. Charlie Shaughnessy is speakable. David's name is OK for an actor; it has a sort of rhythm. Furthermore, as the late Cyril Bennett, Controller of London Weekend TV, once assured me when I was talking about my second son, 'David is a Jewish name. You get places in show business with a Jewish name. That's why I'm called Cyril Bennett.'

In 1970 we moved from our London home in Chelsea to live in Hampshire, and Jean gave up her career as an actress – professional that is – for good, becoming a busy, garden-mad, country wife and mother. She spins about Hampshire in her Mini, meeting trains, taking her garden produce to the WI market in Andover, producing plays for the village drama group, washing, ironing, cooking, feeding the dogs, the cat, the birds, the chickens, getting bathed, dressed and made up in ten minutes flat to drive off to dinner-parties the other side of the county, entertaining guests, shopping, listening to other people's troubles, giving talks to women's organizations – you name it. She is a dynamo of energy and adored by everyone, whoever comes into her orbit – men, women and children alike. She is the prototype warm human being with a big heart. In 1973 we celebrated our silver wedding anniversary and it 'didn't seem a day too much'.

How strange that chance involvement with a friend in staging

9   Deauville, 1937. *L* to *r*: John Mills, the author, Isadore Kerman, Frances Day, Tony Pelissier.

10   Three bearers of famous military names: Earl Haig, Valerian Wellesley (now Duke of Wellington), Earl of Uxbridge (now Marquess of Anglesey), with Lady Caroline Paget and the author. Plas Newydd, 1938.

11   The author with Frances Day at Blackpool Airport, 1937.

12   The author as an ensign in the Grenadier Guards, 1940.

13 The author with Guardsman Ford. Holland, 1944.

14 Rex Whistler's drawing on the wall of the author's hut.

15 The Princesses visit Ealing Studios. *L* to *r*: Reginald Baker, the author, Princess Elizabeth, Miss Crawford, Michael Balcon, Princess Margaret.

16 *Brandy for the Parson. L* to *r*: Michael Trubshawe, Jean Lodge, Charles Hawtrey, James Donald.

17 *Cat Girl. L* to *r*: Ernest Milton, Lily Kann, Barbara Shelley.

18 John Salew as 'Mother Goose' in *The Impersonator.*

a small charity revue in a Berkshire village could have steered me into a situation which gave me a lifetime of exquisite happiness and enabled me to bask in the rare luxury of a wonderful marriage, blessed with two splendid sons. No man could ask for more and I can only hope that my happiness has been shared.

— THIRTEEN —

Stars in Close-Up

In the winter of 1948, while I was still a dogsbody at Ealing Studios, Charlie Frend's film *Scott of the Antarctic* was chosen for the annual Royal Film Performance in aid of the Cinematograph Trade Benevolent Fund.

Mick Balcon, knowing the evening would also traditionally incorporate personal appearances by many invited film stars, suggested that the film should be preceded by a properly written and produced stage revue in which the internationally famous stars would take part – rather than an embarrassing series of walk-ons and bows. Jack Hulbert was invited to stage such a show and I was detailed to work with Jack on the script. We were given the George Mitchell Choir, a full-scale theatre orchestra to work with and, of course, the stars.

I suggested a front-cloth opening of the entrance to the Empire Cinema, Leicester Square, where we were, with the choir dressed as a surging mob of fans trying to get in to see the stars and being held back by friendly policemen and commissionaires. For this I wrote a fast, breathless opening number and as it ended the front-cloth flew away to reveal an exact replica of the foyer of the Empire where the stars were introduced. We teamed them up, in groups, so that they could play out little rehearsed scenes and sketches before going off into their seats in the 'cinema', as it were.

For the first time, I believe, the show was slick, well-rehearsed and entertaining, and Jack and I received some kudos – me for my script, Jack for his smooth production. So, the following year, when the chosen Royal Command film was a fairly gruesome Hollywood version of the *Forsyte Saga* with Errol Flynn, Greer Garson and Walter Pidgeon, Jack Hulbert and I were once again asked to put on a stage show.

This time, encouraged by the previous year's entertainment and feeling a little more ambitious, we hit on the idea of making the whole thing into part of a pantomime. The idea was to start off with a conventional 'Cinderella' kitchen scene – cast, of course, with stars – and eventually go into the big ballroom set to find the rest of the stars as guests at the ball. Here again we contrived little sketches, quartets, duologues for them to do within the context of Cinderella's ball.

Most of the book and the music of *Cinderella* were brilliantly written by Phil Park, a master of pantomime. I again devised and wrote much of the stars' material, which I was lucky enough to rehearse with them in the few weeks preceding the show in various hotel rooms and corners of film studios.

I doubt if any production of *Cinderella* ever had such a cast: Prince Charming was Gregory Peck; Cinderella was Jean Simmons; Buttons: Dickie Attenborough; Fairy Godmother: Moira Lister; Demon King: Sir Ralph Richardson.

Much of the fun with the stars' sketches came from the chemistry of putting unlikely people together. In one little three-handed piece I wrote for the first Royal Film Performance the cast was Rosalind Russell, Michael Wilding and Gregory Peck. In another sketch Ralph Richardson appeared with the blonde bombshell Virginia Mayo. Other great stars of the day in the two shows I worked on were Myrna Loy, Elizabeth Taylor, who did a sketch with Robert Taylor, Ronald Reagan, Robert Donat, Greer Garson, Irene Dunne, Vivien Leigh, Laurence Olivier and Ann Sothern

My happiest contribution, I think, was after Jack Hulbert had said to me one day while we were planning the 1948 show: 'What are we going to do with Alec Guinness?' I went away and thought hard. An idea struck me, so I went back to Jack the next day. This was the result:

At some point in the show, Ben Lyon, who was the compere, came on stage and, lowering his voice to produce a more serious and respectful atmosphere, gave the following speech: 'Your Majesties, Your Royal Highnesses, My Lords, Ladies and Gentlemen, as you know this performance is given in aid of the Cinematograph Trade Benevolent Fund, which takes care of a number of old and infirm former film technicians at its rest home, Glebelands. Here men who have in their time helped to put British films on the map, skilled craftsmen of the camera who have seen better days or fallen on hard times, find rest and comfort in their old age. We thought it appropriate therefore to invite along tonight to join us here one of the very oldest and most senior of the early British film technicians. He was making silent pictures in the 1900s under George Pearson and he's travelled all the way down from Wolverhampton to be with us tonight. I take great pleasure in introducing to you . . . Herbert. . . .'

To polite, warm applause and murmurs of affection and sympathy an old man shuffled onto the stage blinking at the footlights and wearing a moth-eaten dinner-jacket, stick-up collar and steel-rimmed glasses. Ben proceeded to interview him. At first the little man was shy and Ben had to help get the mike closer to him. Ben asked him how long he'd been in films, all about the old days when the camera was cranked by hand and then he said: 'Tell me, Herbert, what do you think of the film stars of today, compared with those of your day, I mean people like Henry Edwardes, Carl Brisson, Mabel Poulton.' Herbert replied: 'Some of 'em are all right . . . there's that . . . what's 'is name . . . Larry Oliver, is it? He's a good 'un . . . yes. . . .'

A slight, kindly laugh but still the deferential, warm affection for the old timer. At last the interview was over and the old technician started to walk off, as Ben said: 'Well, thank you for joining us and good luck and . . . just one moment, Herbert, I quite forgot to ask you your full name. What is your full name?'

The old technician paused, looked round and said in a very matter-of-fact voice: 'My full name, sir, is Herbert Alexander Guinness Crankhandle,' and he was gone. There was a second's silence, then a gasp, then a roar of laughter and thunderous applause.

When I first submitted that idea to Alec Guinness, he liked it – I suppose he was grateful for anything to do other than just walk on and bow – but being a very modest man and with a superb theatrical sense, he could not and would not – as I had proposed – do a sort of dramatic unmasking at the end. That would be showing off. So Guinness himself suggested the compromise exit and it worked a treat.

Needless to say Guinness was miraculous in the detail of observation in the movements and mannerisms of his old film technician from Wolverhampton. He was absolutely real and watching him,

I almost believed in the old man myself, wondering whether Ben had suddenly found someone and brought him on. Recently, when Sir Alec came down to open the new Salisbury Playhouse and I reminded him of that sketch he told me that Ralph Richardson walked right past him that night in the wings and never recognized him.

The great kick of scriptwriting for the Royal Film Performance was the chance to work closely with so many world-famous stars and to observe at close hand their varying degrees of conceit or modesty, of 'troupership' or temperamental nonsense. As most people have noticed, the bigger the star the nicer they are to work with. The more famous the stars were, the harder they worked to co-operate and make the show a success. Some of the lesser British stars we presented, who shall be nameless, showed up badly against the Myrna Loys, Irene Dunnes and Rosalind Russells. They made scenes about their dressing-rooms, their make-up, their costumes, their material. I will be charitable and put it down to nerves. After all, it must have been fairly nerve-wracking to go on stage and compete with the likes of Gregory Peck, Vivien Leigh or Robert Taylor.

It was at the beginning of that 1949 Royal Film Show that there occurred an incident that has since been misreported, so I will set the record straight. The stars were being marshalled in the foyer, ready to be presented to the King and Queen, when Jack Hulbert realized I hadn't been put into the alphabetical line with the stars. So, in a panic, for the Royals were approaching, he told me to go and stand on the extreme right of the line next to Dickie Attenborough.

The King and Queen duly approached, escorted by Reginald Bromhead of the CTBF who was to introduce the stars off a list he had in his hand. As the King came up to me, Reggie Bromhead in a clear voice called out: 'Mr Richard Attenborough.' To which the King said: 'That's not Attenborough, that's Shaughnessy; I know him.'

The press picked up the incident and the next day's *Express* ran a photograph of me beside one of Dickie Attenborough with a rather silly piece about the film star and the courtier's scriptwriter stepson being mistaken for one another. I was delighted. It was good publicity for me at that time to be called a scriptwriter of any sort. And in the *Daily Express* too!

In 1951 the movie world was intrigued by the formation of a new production company called Group Three, backed by NFFC funds and to be run jointly by veteran film-maker John Baxter and John Grierson, the father of documentary. Mick Balcon was to supervise the overall operation with James Lawrie of the Film Bank responsible for the finance. The brief was to try out new young directors, writers and producers on low-budget films of quality and originality.

After I had finished a stint as personal assistant to Thorold Dickinson on *Secret People* I was going spare and so was John Eldridge, a talented young documentary director who had won acclaim for *Three Dawns to Sydney* and *The Waverley Steps*. Eldridge and I decided to get hold of a subject and persuade Balcon to let us make it.

Among the unmade scripts lying on the dusty shelves at Ealing was a version of Geoffrey Household's *Brandy for the Parson*, an hilarious novel about three young people smuggling brandy over from France in a yacht and transporting it across country to London on the backs of pack ponies in the old eighteenth-century style. As scripted the film would have been too costly for Group Three, so John and I scaled it all down. I re-wrote the screenplay entirely and Mick Balcon, glad to get shot of a 'dead' Ealing subject, gave the go-ahead. Locations in Devon and Dorset were found. Then John and I had to face the problem of casting the three star parts: Bill Harper, the orthodox young man on holiday; Petronilla, his girlfriend; and Tony Rackham, the debonair young adventurer who gets them involved in the smuggling operation.

Group Three's policy was to find unknown players and make them into stars. But I wanted something in the way of marquee names, be it minor ones whom we could afford. I was offered James Donald, then a big name in films, who had just *not* done *Androcles and the Lion* in Hollywood, was home, bored, and wanting a working holiday. His price was out of the question but the magic name of Grierson, coupled with the prospect of a yachting holiday in Devon with his wife and stepchild, made him instantly amenable and I got him for a special fee.

John and I had been chatting up Audrey Hepburn, who was just becoming much talked about, and urging her to play Petronilla. She was in *Secret People* so we were seeing her at the studio most days. She had followed the progress of our script with interest, and said she would be delighted to do our picture next. When the script was ready I gave her the first draft to read and she handed it back to me the following day with a sweet but mischievous smile. 'Lovely,' she said, 'but I couldn't play Scene 42. The censor wouldn't allow it.'

I grabbed my harmless, innocent and thoroughly wholesome script from her hands and tore through the pages. Scene 42? It read as follows:

Scene 42. INT. CABIN OF YACHT. DAY. (STUDIO)
Petronilla is awake, dressed in Bill's pyjamas. *She is peeing out of the porthole.*

The ladies in the script-typing pool had omitted the letter 'r', either by accident or design.

As the weeks went by John and I prepared every detail of our film but Group Three failed to approve the budget. There were discussions in progress and it looked all right. But until we had the final OK from the company, I could not make contracts. Audrey's agent, Kenneth Harper, kept on ringing me for news but I could not commit myself. One day Harper rang to say that he'd had an offer for Audrey to go down to Monte Carlo and play in a film with a bandleader called Ray Ventura. It was a nothing part but she was to have a Dior dress, the money was good, and it would mean a month in the sun. Nevertheless, she'd still rather do *Brandy for the Parson*. I pointed this little pistol at Group Three's head but they still couldn't give me a start date or a commitment. So Audrey had to go. John and I were shattered. Later, when we'd started the picture, I had a postcard from her from Monte Carlo saying how sad she was not to be with us, 'especially as I hear you've got the lovely James Donald' or words to that effect.

But the strange fates that often affect people's lives were at work that summer in the Principality of Monaco. Sitting in the foyer of Audrey's hotel in Monte Carlo one evening was an old woman, who sent a waiter over to Audrey, just come in from filming and about to go upstairs in the lift.

'The lady just inside the door would like to speak to you, Mademoiselle.' Audrey, who always had impeccable manners, instantly complied. The old woman smiled. 'Sit down, my dear child, and talk to me. I think you are my Gigi.'

Of course it was Colette and the stage version (straight, not musical) of *Gigi* was to go into rehearsal in New York that autumn. Of course Audrey got the part and of course she took Broadway by storm as Gigi, was film-tested in Hollywood, did *Roman Holiday* with William Wyler and was soon away to world stardom. I often reflect that had Audrey come down with us to Devon and played the not very rewarding part of Petronilla, her break might have been longer coming. But come it would have, in the end, for she had dazzling, devastating star quality, even in the chorus line of *Sauce Tartare* at the Cambridge Theatre, for you couldn't look at anyone else on that crowded stage.

After losing Audrey Hepburn we tested a number of other young ladies for Petronilla and among them, at John Eldridge's suggestion, my wife, Jean Lodge. Her test was so much better than the others that John and our production supervisor, the experienced and notable Isobel Pargiter ('Pargie' to many film folk) advised me to cast her. Grierson agreed. So I did.

Most people who know about films know about John Grierson. He was a Scot and the 'father of documentary'. He is said to have invented the term 'documentary film'. When John Eldridge and I went under contract to Group Three Films, we came under the command of Grierson, who had been appointed Joint Executive in charge of Production. John already knew Grierson slightly. I had never met him and my first encounter with the great man was in his tiny office at Southall Studios, where he was sitting with both feet on the desk, picking his teeth and talking with what I took to be an American accent. He gave the impression of a rep actor playing the part of a Hollywood tycoon.

He was on the phone saying, 'Yeah . . . yeah . . . have the boy come and talk to me. . . . Yeah . . . it's a load of shit . . . but it's got style and impudence . . . we'll do it. . . .'

I later discovered that he was really speaking with his native Scots accent, which had become mildly transatlanticized through working in Canada.

Grierson was either a genius or the biggest phoney ever. I'm still not sure. He had a gift for finding the most unlikely but somehow remarkable phrases for describing things, be it a story idea, a piece of music, a whole picture, a shot, even a cut. He was a master of what I call 'give it to me pear-shaped' talk. He would sit watching our rushes in the projection theatre and make these strange pronouncements on our work. He called *Brandy for the Parson* 'a

sweet lemon of a picture', which was nice and apt; later he dubbed
it 'W. W. Jacobs pretty' and added that it had the feel of 'old oak
and seaweed'.

His analytical utterings were peppered with phrases about two-
tier textures, master tones, simulated behaviour patterns and God
knows what, but he always conveyed what he meant in a sort of
abstract way. Of course, he really detested the 'commercial'
cinema, just as many drama people hate the 'commercial' theatre.
He had plenty of time for Pabst, Buñuel and Jean Vigo but very
little for Carol Reed, David Lean or Hitchcock. Like all docu-
mentary-minded film-makers, Grierson loved the realism of ordinary people on film, non-actors, photographed dramatically against
a brooding sky; the lined, granite faces of very old weather-beaten
North Sea fishermen, ploughmen, shepherds, railway signalmen,
Covent Garden porters and so on. He had a sort of contempt for
actors in films and a deep distrust of the artifice of film studios and
sets.

It must have been quite an act of self-betrayal for him to supervise the production of a programme of entertainment films with
fictional stories and actors in them, produced in studios with manu-
factured sets and elaborate lighting. But he undertook it and
found all sorts of wonderful, intellectual reasons for being so employed. He was pulling British films away from 'phoney Park Lane
drawing-rooms into the real world of gut and bowel and vomit,' or
so he told himself.

One day, when I was casting *Laxdale Hall,* my film of Eric
Linklater's novel, I went into Grierson's office with a copy of *Spotlight,* the actors' and actresses' *Who's Who,* to show him the photograph of a player I was keen to engage for a fairly important role
in the picture. Grierson took the *Spotlight* from me, glanced at it
and, although it weighed a ton, hurled it with fury against the wall
of his office, shouting, 'That's what's the matter with goddam
British movies!'

Later on he allowed me to engage Ronald Squire to play an
ageing Scottish laird, sanctioning his permission by saying: 'I guess
Squire's Englishness against a Highland background will be like
a 'cello playing against the orchestra in a different key and give us
a disturbing excitement of the aural and visual senses.' It was cer-
tainly one way of looking at it.

John Grierson's great gift was that of enthusing people with what they were doing and helping them to see beyond the immediate mundane task into a realm of high artistic and aesthetic endeavour. I don't think he was entirely happy at Group Three, but it was a pleasure and an education to work with him.

For the part of Tony Rackham in *Brandy for the Parson* I wanted Guy Middleton, who was ideal. But Balcon and Grierson said we must play someone a little less well-known and obvious, since experiment was the keynote of Group Three films. I sulked about that and rather gave up. Eventually, Stanley Dubens, who was my agent at the time, said: 'What about Kenneth More?' I'd seen Kenny in a couple of small parts in films. He was an eye-catching actor but not a 'name' and I was indifferent. Stanley said: 'At least get him down and test him.' So we did. In due course this breezy, happy-go-lucky chap turned up at Southall Studios in a small red sports car, strolled onto the set, never seemed to look at his script once and sailed through the test scene with such ease and effortless charm that we started talking wardrobe and dates to him before the test had been unloaded from the magazine to go off to the labs.

So we lost one potential star in Audrey but gained another in Kenny. And I've enjoyed Kenny's friendship ever since. He has two of the most attractive qualities an actor can have: great generosity and loyalty to old friends. I think he has always had a soft spot for that funny, happy little picture we all made in our youth down at Salcombe and on the Dorset Downs. It was the first film with his name over the title and we did have tremendous fun.

The cast was rich in talent: James Donald, Charles Hawtrey as a simple-minded laundry-van driver, Alfie Bass, Arthur Wontner, a distinguished old-timer, Mike Trubshawe, Freddie Piper and others. Mike Trubshawe played an eccentric gentleman farmer, in whose house on the downs the three adventurers are invited to shelter for the night from a storm. Older filmgoers will know that for years David Niven used to work Trubshawe's name into his pictures as something between a lucky charm and a salute to his lifelong friend. In *Brandy* Mike was able to return the compliment.

As Petronilla, Tony and Bill staggered, dripping wet, into the farmhouse, I wrote the following line for Mike: 'Make yourselves at home and I'll get Mrs Niven to run you a bath.' It got a nice laugh at the press show.

The highly original musical score for *Brandy* was composed and conducted by John Addison, who went on to great heights in the film and theatre music world. In a sense we were all beginners on that film and it was acclaimed by the critics both here and in the USA as a 'triumph of youth'. Because Group Three was wholly financed by Government money through the National Film Finance Corporation and *Brandy* was the first picture produced under the scheme, the *News Chronicle* notice was headlined: 'Whitehall Blazes the Trail'. Thus John and I, with our first feature film, had played a small part in British cinema history.

— FOURTEEN —

Making Movies

Following the success of *Brandy for the Parson* Eldridge and I started looking for another so-called 'regional' comedy with which to make another film. Some months previously one of the Ealing directors, Charles Crichton, had announced at a production meeting that as a dedicated fisherman he longed to make a film about salmon poaching in Scotland. Eric Linklater, the most distinguished Scottish author anyone could think of after Compton Mackenzie (whose *Whisky Galore* Ealing had recently filmed), was then approached and offered a substantial fee to write a salmon poaching story for Charlie to film.

Linklater wrote a few pages and delivered. I never saw his story outline. It was none of my business. All I know is that it was read and minds were changed. Charlie's salmon poaching idea was abandoned. Linklater then asked for his storyline back, that is, he requested that the rights in it should revert to him, although he had been paid to write it. His offer was that, given his story back, he would turn it into a new novel and that, on publication, Ealing Studios would automatically own the film rights in the novel.

All was agreed. John Eldridge and I came into the story at a point when Mick Balcon found he had on his hands the film rights in a new Eric Linklater novel and nobody at Ealing wanted to film it. John and I did and were immediately given the go-ahead to prepare *Laxdale Hall* for a Group Three production. It was a difficult novel to adapt. Linklater had surrounded his very funny basic story of a revolt by a tiny Highland community against Whitehall interference with pages and pages of classical parallels, philosophy and intellectual diatribe. For example, in the book, the Highland villagers put on a Greek play for the MPs' visit from London and

120

there are all sorts of hidden references to the modern situation in the classical narrative. We simplified this for the film to an open-air production of *Macbeth*.

I did preserve much of Linklater's quaint Highland dialogue and used some of his descriptive material in an early scene in the House of Commons, when a young official from the Scottish Office is briefing the Parliamentary mission about the wild, outlandish place. This enabled me to establish the place and the main characters before the mission landed off the steamer and the story proper began.

After a terrific battle with Grierson, I finally cast Ronnie Squire as General Mathieson, the old laird of Laxdale. The three men from Westminster were Raymond Huntley as Pettigrew, Sebastian Shaw as Hugh Marvell and Fulton Mackay as Flett, the young ex-schoolmaster from the Scottish Office. He and Prunella Scales, whose first film job this was, provided the young romantic interest. The rest of the cast were mostly Glasgow Citizens Theatre players and many of them have since made their names: Andrew Keir, Roddy MacMillan, James Gilbert, James Copeland, Rikki Fulton and others. The part of General Mathieson's daughter, Catriona, set me a special problem. I wanted an attractive, country-bred girl of twenty-five or twenty-six; not a Mayfair ex-debutante but a girl born and bred in the Highlands with a faint Highland Scots accent. I also wanted an actress with a bit of a name to help sell the picture, but there were no 'marquee' names who were suitable for the part, that we could afford on our modest budget.

One Sunday morning during the film's preparation period, I went to Mass, as was my wont, at the Brompton Oratory. Jean was with me. I sat there and thought about my casting problem. I cannot claim to have asked Our Lady in prayer to solve the problem for me but I was pondering over the casting of Catriona as the Mass began.

Suddenly there was a shuffling in the pew immediately in front of us and a tall, dark and very beautiful girl in dark glasses, wearing a good quality tweed coat and skirt with a little chiffon scarf at her neck and one over her head, edged her way over the legs of those kneeling in the pew in front to reach an inside seat beside a column inches from my nose. For a long time I couldn't see her face. All through the Confiteor, the Gospel, Epistle and the sermon I failed to get a look at that face. Something told me I should. It wasn't until after the sermon and the end of the Credo when she turned to kneel for the Sanctus that I caught sight of a gorgeous face that was somehow familiar.

I spent the rest of the Mass wondering where I'd seen the girl before. As we reached the final blessing and the *'Ite, missa est'* I suddenly got it. She was a film actress, Irish, called Kathleen Ryan. I'd seen her in Carol Reed's film *Odd Man Out*; also in Launder and Gilliat's *Captain Boycott*. I hadn't seen her in anything else for some time and had a vague idea I'd read somewhere that she was married to a Dublin vet, didn't really want a film career and had given up.

Nothing daunted I followed her through the throng pouring out of the Oratory, leaving Jean floundering behind. I caught up with my quarry on the church steps and daringly grasped her arm.

'Excuse me,' I gasped, out of breath, 'but are you Kathleen Ryan?' 'To be sure I am,' I think she said (or perhaps it was only what I wanted her to say). In a matter of seconds I had established that she was still available for films, no one had offered her a job lately, she'd adore to read the script of *Laxdale Hall* and her agent was Al Parker. So I telephoned Ronnie Waters at the Al Parker office first thing on the Monday morning. A deal was agreed and I had my leading lady. A miracle?

Laxdale Hall was a gruelling picture to make, the location being an utterly wild and remote place called Applecross on the West Coast opposite Skye. The camera crew and director were billeted in crofts in the village itself, while the rest of the unit travelled every single morning at seven o'clock over a formidable mountain pass in a small fleet of four-wheel-drive taxis hired from Inverness. At Applecross itself conditions were even harder and we all got soaked to the skin every day and exhausted from humping equipment over rocks and rivers. John Eldridge, the lighting cameraman, Arthur Grant and I twice had to drive forty-three miles after the day's filming to see our rushes in a broken-down fleapit of a cinema at Achnasheen. This followed sinister reports from the labs in London. But all was well and we returned eventually to complete the interiors in the studios at Southall.

Linklater loved our film of his book when it appeared in 1954 and wrote to Mick Balcon in praise of our work. The picture had a particular success in Scotland, naturally, since its theme was essentially Scottish Nationalist in flavour and the film presented a fairly truthful Scotland with real, believable Highland characters living their lives in their environment. Not some bogus, Hollywood, 'Brigadoon' kind of Scotland with bagpipes, haggis, kilts and old men with crooked walking-sticks looking like Sir Harry Lauder playing the Holborn Empire.

Laxdale Hall was to be, alas, my last feature film with John Eldridge. He made one more film for Group Three, *Conflict of Wings,* and so did I: *The End of the Road,* a worthy, touching little picture about an old factory worker facing the problems of retirement. He was played by dear old Finlay Currie and Wolf Rilla directed.

Soon after Group Three folded in 1954 John and I lost touch. We met again in 1959, my year at J. Walter Thomson's. We found ourselves working together as director and advertising producer on a promotional film for the Cheese Board. Not long after the cheese film I heard that John had finally lost his long and bravely fought battle against the TB that had wrecked his lungs and put a huge strain on his heart. He died far too young. Yet, in a curious way, it seemed inevitable. He had the soul of a poet and his sense of visual beauty was rare. He was the classic consumptive young poet, who wastes away in a Victorian novel. He was a film poet, leaving behind him some beautiful, evocative work in the medium he loved.

It had long been clear to me that in films everyone wants to direct. Just as every soldier has a field-marshal's baton in his knapsack, so every cutter, assistant director and production manager carries a director's view-finder in his briefcase. When you are directing a film your status in the studio is very high indeed. On your own set, you're called 'Guv' and endless people bring you coffee and sandwiches and consult you on a variety of problems as you sit supremely in charge in a canvas chair with your name on it. All the innumerable people on the set – actors, technicians, carpenters, hairdressers, make-up girls, painters, electricians, prop men and so on – are under your orders. You are the general in command of the battle and what you say goes.

You can glide gracefully up on the crane with your camera operator and look down from a height on all the grovelling yesmen below. Everybody looks up – literally – to hear what you're going to say. The sense of power is irresistible.

If you suddenly look through the camera and say in a loud voice: 'I can't shoot on that set, the rostrum's too high and the walls are too low,' in theory someone will give an immediate order for the set to be dismantled, while the cast retire to their dressing rooms and a labour force of chippies and painters will virtually rebuild the set – even if it takes until the next afternoon.

In practice, mercifully, this doesn't happen – at least not nowadays – even with big-time film-makers such as David Lean, Otto Preminger or Hitchcock. Today such giants of the cinema are their own producers and as such must be concerned with the economics of their own films, upon whose earnings at the box-office their livelihood depends.

I had been a producer of films before I became a director. Up to 1956 I had written movie scripts and on one or two occasions had produced the films I had written, working with a director. I'd worked twice with John Eldridge, once with Wolf Rilla, and once with Clive Donner (*Heart of a Child*). I had also written a screenplay from a stage play by the Welsh author E. Eynon Evans called *Bless This House* and under the new title of *Room in the House* the film was made for A.C.T. Films, the trade union producing unit, with me as producer and that veteran of hundreds of films, Maurice Elvey, then in his seventies, as director.

As a result of this quite successful little comedy, in which incidentally I believe I gave Billie Whitelaw her first ever part in a film, I was approached again by A.C.T. Films to re-script and produce a thriller called *Suspended Alibi*. The script needed work and I knew I had a little power in my hand. A.C.T. were committed to making the picture, having booked stage space at Walton Studios for a firm starting date. So I took a deep breath and told Ralph Bond of A.C.T. Films that I would be delighted to revise the script but only on condition that I could direct the picture and not produce it. There was a momentary silence. 'I'll have to think about that,' he said. Discussions were held. I had never directed before but I thought I knew how and was quite capable of saying 'Action' and 'Cut' in a loud, confident voice. After a day or two I was informed that the board of A.C.T. Films, of which an old pre-war friend, Anthony Asquith, was chairman, had agreed. I was in. I was a film director.

I rang up Puffin Asquith and thanked him profusely for the break then set about preparing my picture with consummate care. I knew the script well, of course, having written it and I drew all the usual diagrams and hieroglyphics all over each page, as I envisaged each camera set-up in minute detail.

The set to be used for the first two days of the film was already built and virtually dressed by the Friday afternoon before the Monday when shooting was due to start. So I went down to the studio on the Saturday, quite alone, with my script all marked and ready and managed to get onto the appropriate stage by conning the fireman. There I walked about the set, imagining every camera position exactly, playing the scenes to myself, deciding where to cover with close-ups, where to pan, where to track the camera. . . .

On the Monday morning I knew so exactly what I intended to do that there was no delay in starting. As soon as the actors came on the set, made up and ready to rehearse, we were off and the first set-up was in the can by half-past nine.

My leading lady in *Suspended Alibi* was Honor Blackman, who had just returned from an unhappy time in Canada and was at a low ebb in her fortunes. She was forced at that time to play in endless grotty second-features like mine. But Honor is a tremendous professional. She was so good and so helpful and easy to work with that I fell madly in love with her and have loved her in a warm but respectable way ever since. She became a great friend of my wife's and mine and it was most gratifying to see her go soaring back to the top of the tree, where she rightly belonged, in the years that followed.

The next picture I directed was a horror movie and it came about when I was under contract to the Rank Organization at Pinewood but on loan to Sydney Box and Peter Rogers at Beaconsfield Studios. An American company called American International Pictures had a deal to co-finance with Stuart Levy and Nat Cohen of Anglo-Amalgamated a script by an American writer, called *Cat Girl.* It was a sort of joke around Beaconsfield Studios. Peter Rogers had instructions from Sydney to make it; nobody wanted to direct it. So, keen as mustard to direct another film, I took a pace forward. The film was mine.

The script, however, was awful, so I rewrote it from start to finish and in so doing tried to rationalize the weird obsession held by the beautiful leading lady, Leonora, that she was really a leopard. The original script made no bones about it. She actually turned into a leopard at night, when the moon was full. There were to be shots of her wrists becoming hairy and her face snarling – by successive matching dissolves – into a feline monster.

I altered all this hokum and in my version of the script implied that the illusion was in her mind and that she was a psychiatric case. However, in her close mental association with a leopard, she actually controlled with her mind the actions of a wild leopard that lurked about in the woods. It became her alter ego. The film was shot in three hysterical weeks with the gorgeous Barbara Shelley starring in her first picture. By using her, at Sydney Box's suggestion – for he had placed her under contract – I fear we condemned a very beautiful and talented actress to a long career in horror films, from which she has now mercifully escaped.

For the major role of the Cat Girl's evil, insane uncle I had the honour to work with Ernest Milton, one of our greatest Shakespearian actors, whom I had seen play Shylock when I was a schoolboy. He was almost forgotten when he came down to play in my film but the strangely high-fluting, precious voice and the flashing eyes were most effective. In one shot he had to walk across the set with the leopard at his heels. Petrified, he asked me to release him from this dangerous task. 'If I get a nip on the ankle I shall forget my lines,' he said. So we put Ernest's trousers on the leopard's trainer and took the shot from ground level, following the animal with 'doubled' legs.

Cat Girl was made in 1957 when the new X-certificate was enabling the makers of what were even then known as 'exploitation' films to combine the ingredients of erotic sex and violent horror in the same picture. My brief was to achieve just this. However, there was still a limit beyond which the censor would not allow a director to go on both counts – otherwise he could withhold any kind of certificate.

So we used to shoot both a British and a Continental version of all naughty scenes. If a girl had her dress ripped off in the British version, she was normally left with a neat, well-laundered C & A bra underneath. For the Continental version, the bra was left off and if the actress didn't fancy being bare to the waist, a double with a bust of like proportions was engaged to stand in for the close shot.

When I first worked at Ealing Studios the American code was in full force and Joseph Breen was setting a standard of near absurdity in movie decency. In *Saraband for Dead Lovers* I recall that Basil Dearden, the director, was told he could shoot the boudoir scene as scripted on the condition that if Joan Greenwood was lying prone on the couch, Stewart Granger could have his tunic off but *must* have his feet touching the ground. Alternatively Mr Granger could also be lying prone on another couch across the room, but in that case his tunic must be on.

Robert Hamer received back his script for *It Always Rains on Sunday* from the British Board of Film Censors with a letter stating that, since there were three 'bloodies' and four 'bleedings' in it, he could either use all the 'bloodies' but no 'bleedings', or reduce the number of both by 50 per cent. Imagine such prudery in any film today – least of all a British one ! I did a shot in *Cat Girl* of Barbara Shelley sitting up in bed suddenly as a sinister German housekeeper barges into her room with a candle in the middle of the night. I set up the camera behind Barbara's head (she'd gone to bed, needless to say, in her birthday suit, as it was a warm night) so that as she sat up into shot we could delight the customers with a large expanse of the star's lovely naked back. But my camera operator, who knew the censor's rules 'back to front', said they'd only accept it down to the third vertebra from the sacrum. So at Barbara's own suggestion the make-up girl drew a line with a lipstick across her back for the camera operator to use as his bottom-of-frame limit. A second lipstick line was drawn so low as to traverse Barbara's behind. That was the framing line for the Continental version. A hilarious afternoon on the set for all.

It came as a great surprise to me – for I had no very high opinion myself of *Cat Girl* – when a book was recently published called *A Heritage of Horror* by David Pirie. This was a sort of compendium of British-made gothic horror pictures and it singled out *Cat Girl* as a landmark in the development of British horror movies, praising it and taking it really quite seriously as a piece of cinema art. It was later shown in a special season of gothic horror pictures at the National Film Theatre.

I could hardly believe my eyes when I read, in Pirie's chapter about *Cat Girl:* 'Unfortunately Alfred Shaughnessy never made another horror film after *Cat Girl.*' It was as though the great master had turned his hand to another genre. The truth was that after *Cat Girl,* nobody asked me to direct anything, until Sydney Box got another deal with Anglo-Amalgamated to put together a rock-and-roll movie, *Six-Five Special,* aimed at exploiting the sudden upsurge in pop music and the TV show of the same name. Once again, nobody wanted to direct it. I would have directed a nature film about insects, a slapstick silent, the telephone book, anything at all. So I stepped forward again.

Six-Five Special was a weekly television programme in which teenage fans crowded the studios and were televised jigging about and reacting with ecstasy to the various pop acts and groups performing on a rostrum. The show was compered by Pete Murray and Josephine Douglas. The film was seen at the outset as a chance to put on the screen in one picture most of the outstanding pop acts of the day. These included Dickie Valentine, Lonnie Donnegan, Joan Regan, Johnny Dankworth and his Orchestra with Cleo Laine, The King Brothers, Jim Dale, The Kentones, Diane Todd, Jimmy Lloyd, Petula Clark and many others.

The plot was simple. Two stage-struck provincial girls, played by Diane Todd and Avril Leslie, decide to travel to London and try to break into show business, the one as a singer, the other as her manager. They go to some unspecified railway station and board a train, due to leave at 6.5. The train (shades of *Jazz Train*) is packed with celebrities, singers and performers of all kinds travelling to London. It was pure fantasy; the train symbolized the girls' ambitions, the railroad to success.

Once on board, the two girls walked down the length of the train, finding famous stars rehearsing in compartments, sleeping cars, in the restaurant car, the luggage van and the corridors. They marvelled at what they saw. The second half of the picture was set in the TV studio, where the singing girl got a part in the chorus – it was a start – and we saw through the girls' eyes the whole exciting technical operation of a big musical TV show going on the air live.

There were masses of good musical numbers in the film, especially 'Baby Lover', which was written specially for Pet Clark by Tony Hatch. A rather swoony number of my own was slipped in as a director's perk. It was called 'You Are My Favourite Dream' and was sung in her screen bath by Diane Todd, to a lush orchestral backing by Geoff Love, which made me feel for a few magic weeks as though I was Jerome Kern himself.

In essence, directing *Six-Five Special* was a question of thinking up new, untried ways of screening a musical act. A lot of the shots, as the numbers were played, were reaction shots of the teenagers screaming, jumping about and tapping their feet. I had dozens of genuine pop fans in the studio for this purpose.

One morning as we were about to shoot a big musical number, someone said the studios had become a bit hot and stuffy, so we had the big air extractors switched on to ventilate the place. When the red light eventually flashed and the shooting bell clanged, the assistant called out, 'Quiet now, please, stand by to shoot and kill the fans.' Needless to say, this was greeted with gales of youthful laughter from our teenage crowd.

When, in 1959, James Archibald gave up his post as head of production at the J. Arthur Rank film studios at Pinewood, he was snapped up by J. Walter Thompson's, the mammoth international advertising agency, to head the TV and film advertising department of its London office in Berkeley Square. Up to that moment cinema advertising and TV commercials had been produced in the main by small specialist companies, employing technicians not normally engaged in major feature film production. James changed all this.

A slump in the feature industry at that time, causing no small redundancy among leading producers, directors, lighting cameramen and other technical grades gave James the chance to bring a number of these people into the advertising field. Augusta Films, founded by Joseph Janni and Jack Lee, who had scored a great hit with *A Town Like Alice,* was the first company formed around such people.

It soon became possible to tell, for instance, a leading soap manufacturer that in future his precious pink tablets would be photographed by Georges Perinal, who had photographed *La Kermesse Heroique* and most of Korda's pre-war epics, or by Jack Cardiff, or by Robert Krasker, who had lit *The Third Man.* Or that thirty-second TV commercial showing two kids drinking orange juice on a garden seat could, if the agency so chose, be directed by Michael Powell, or Jack Lee, or Karel Reisz. The idea was to dazzle the advertisers with these great and famous names. By and large it worked.

My own contract at Pinewood having lapsed, James Archibald invited me to join him at JWT as one of his film and TV producers. I was to be in charge of the film and television advertising of certain of the agency's accounts. It was fascinating and revealing to work inside a large agency, but there were terrible moments when my loyalties were torn between my clients and my old film colleagues outside the agency who were making the films. The former were often ignorant, pigheaded and arrogant but had to be pleased at all costs, in case the agency lost the account. There were often problems within the agency, as many of the copywriters, who wrote the film scripts for the commercials, had little knowledge of film-making. The final script John Eldridge and I were given from which to produce a sales film about cheese for the Cheese Board had an opening shot described thus: 'The cameras track and pan over a mountain of cheese. . . .'

Looking back, I realize I was probably temperamentally un-suited for a career in advertising. I recall vividly a scene at which I was present one summer afternoon in a large boardroom in Berkeley Square, which sums up the 'ad game' for me.

Twelve grown men, mostly in their fifties and sixties, all of high rank in the agency or the firm they represented, thus men of some wealth, pinstripe-suited, greying, probably with sons at expensive schools, all of them with chauffeur-driven Bentleys waiting outside, sat with grimly serious expressions for three and a half hours around a polished table. Secretaries were on hand to take notes, tumblers of water and embossed leather blotters were before them. Neither the Security Council of the United Nations nor the Board of the Bank of England during an international monetary crisis could have behaved with more solemn dignity or sense of gravity. At the far end of the polished table stood a man in a white coat. For three and a half hours this wretched man remained on his feet, his hand resting lightly on an object, ready every so often to pick it up, turn it round and put it down again on the table. It was a packet of soap flakes. The meeting had been called to discuss a possible change in the size of the lettering on the packet. This change had, of course, been suggested by the agency and would require the client to up their 'billing' or spending on the product's advertising by a few more hundred thousand pounds in the following year. I have no doubt that this was the result.

After a year I left JWT and decided to go into the production side of filmed advertising. From what I had learnt inside Thompson's, I felt confident of picking up enough business to help run a small production company; very soon I joined up with Anthony Perry, a fellow producer recently redundant from Pinewood.

We brought in with us Charles Frend, the distinguished Ealing Studios director, who had made *The Cruel Sea* and *Scott of the Antarctic* and was ready to have a go at Heinz Baked Beans and Eno's Fruit Salts. He was an old friend of both Perry's and mine. To give our company a touch more prestige still, I asked Kenneth

More to join the Board. Kenny agreed at once – it must have been out of sheer friendship, for there was nothing in it for him – and actually invested a little money in the project. He was always like that, a marvellous friend. Another distinguished film director chum of mine, Guy Hamilton, put in some useful working capital when he too joined us. So we had three good film names on our note-paper and our own enthusiasm.

Over the next four years or so, Eyeline Films became one of the best-known, most reputable little film companies in the field of advertising and documentary film-making in Britain. From our small office in Dean Street, Soho, we made two superb films for Cable and Wireless about the laying of the transatlantic cable beneath the ocean, three small feature films, and literally hundreds of TV commercials and cinema advertising films, including many for Camay Soap, Horlicks, Lux Soap (with film stars such as Claudia Cardinale in Rome and Claire Bloom in London), Persil, Galaxy Chocolate, Capstan Cigarettes and others too numerous to mention.

Eyeline was fun and we made a reasonable living out of it for a while. Soon other companies like ours mushroomed and compe-tition became sharp. We extended our operation to Zurich and I shot a number of commercials over there with our subsidiary for European TV. Perrier Water and Suchard Chocolate were two I can recall making with a Swiss-German crew.

Soon after Anthony Perry left to make a feature film outside the company, I became restless. I've always dodged financial respon-sibility, being no sort of a businessman. I didn't fancy taking the whole thing on my shoulders. Others had joined us by then, in-cluding George H. Brown, the successful feature producer, and we had Harold Orton, a brilliant ex-Rank Organization produc-tion supervisor, as our most active partner. These two were good businessmen and knew what they were doing. So I parted amicably from Eyeline, resigning my seat on the Board but retaining some equity shares, which I still hold. It had been a chapter in my career, a worthwhile experience, no bones broken. I went on my way.

As far as my films go (which was never very far), I've always had a soft spot for *The Impersonator*. It was the only picture I both wrote and directed from a story of my own creation.

I'd always found pantomime dames terribly macabre and slightly sinister. Today, of course, gentlemen performing in drag are ten a penny, and imitation Danny La Rues are a commonplace in pubs and working men's clubs. But in my childhood the elderly broad comedian dressed up in a red wig, red nose, rimless specs and voluminous striped underskirts as Mother Goose or Widow Twankey seemed to me a creature apart. Neither man nor woman. In 1960 this feeling germinated in my mind the idea of a panto-mime dame, who was, off-stage, a psychopathic child murderer. The irony appealed to my sense of drama; an ageing man delight-ing an audience of happy, laughing kids, getting them to sing and cheer and hiss and boo and love him on the stage, only to creep away from the theatre after the show and lurk in the dark alleys or on the towpath to assault and strangle a child. It was an ugly thought. But I developed the story into one of those then fashion-able thrillers in which a small boy witnesses a crime but locks away the secret of the killer's identity in his confused mind until a clever detective finds a way of releasing it.

It sounds dreadfully derivative, of course, but the denouement of my story hinged on the child's curiosity after an older child had said to him at school, 'Mother Goose isn't a lady, silly, it's a man dressed up.' At this point the little boy, feeling cheated, crept out of his mother's house at night, went down to the local theatre and going on stage with the other kids, confronted the comedian and caused him to lose control, panic and after a chase up in the flies of the stage, to be arrested by the police and charged with murder. In the end the little boy's childish illusions about Mother Goose were restored and preserved intact by his young schoolteacher.

The censorship of films being what it was in the 1960s, I even-tually had to abandon the child-killer element and had the ageing comedian strangle the widowed mother of the small boy concerned. Nevertheless, it still worked as a story. The main element was un-altered.

I made *The Impersonator* for Bryanston Films on a minute budget and a three-week schedule at Pinewood Studios. In 1962 all the stages at Pinewood except one were crammed to the walls with enormous, lavish sets for *Cleopatra,* Twentieth Century-Fox's ill-fated epic. The wardrobe was swollen with thousands of Roman and Egyptian costumes and the entire back lot was laid out with palm trees, a vast water tank and Egyptian barges to represent Alexandria Harbour during the Roman occupation. Rouben Mamoulian had just retired from the picture as director and

19 Filming *Laxdale Hall* in Scotland. *L* to *r*: John Eldridge, Kathleen Ryan, John Grierson.

20 The author directing John Dare in *The Impersonator*.

21 Planning a sketch for the Royal Film Performance, 1949. *L* to *r*: Jean Simmons, Jack Hulbert, Harold French, the author, Stewart Granger.

22 Jean Lodge and Kenneth More in *Brandy for the Parson.*

23 Jean with David (left) and Charles in 1959.

24 Jean on the steps of our London house, 1969.

25 The author with David Langton, Lesley-Anne Down and Rachel Gurney at the 'Upstairs, Downstairs' fête, Ringwold House, 1975.

26 The author with Jenny Tomasin (Ruby), Karen Dotrice (Lily), Angela Baddeley (Mrs Bridges) and Jean Marsh (Rose) at an *Upstairs, Downstairs* recording in 1975.

Joseph L. Mankiewicz had arrived in the UK to take over.

Elizabeth Taylor was still playing Cleopatra and Burton was her Mark Antony but Caesar (later Rex Harrison) was at that point Peter Finch, who was hanging around Pinewood in his toga, bored to death, while huge crowd scenes were being filmed on the lot with Roman horsemen trotting under a triumphal arch.

The only corner of Pinewood not allocated to *Cleopatra* was the medium-sized G stage and it was rented on special terms for *The Impersonator*.

On the Monday that we started shooting, the *Cleopatra* unit were rehearsing a shot of Roman cavalry trotting through the triumphal arch in a blaze of blue arc lamps and with dozens of assistant directors tearing about yelling through megaphones. Mankiewicz was high up on the Transatlantic crane, smoking a cigar and wearing a tinted eyeshade. It was the full Hollywood bit.

Three weeks later to the day, when we completed our last set-up at Pinewood, the *Cleopatra* unit were just starting to roll cameras on the shot they'd been rehearsing the day we started in the studio. I dare say that scene was finally in the can by the day we had a final cut of our picture.

We were very much the poor relations during those three weeks at Pinewood, struggling on a low budget and shooting at great speed with much enforced economy. One night we used a back gate of the studio, dressed up to represent the entrance to an American Air Force camp in the North of England. We could only just light the setting with our limited number of lamps but there was night shooting in progress across on the Alexandria Harbour lot that night, so the sky was ablaze with light. Much of it spilled over our way and helped us quite a bit.

I shot all my pantomime scenes for *The Impersonator* in the old Metropolitan Theatre, Edgware Road, now alas demolished. It was a lovely, old-fashioned, gilt and plush music hall. When I went in one afternoon to have a look at the place, I found a wrestling ring on the stage and two beefy chaps writhing, grunting and thumping each other on the mat. I said: 'Sorry to interrupt your fight.' One of them looked up at me, his sweaty face framed between the other man's legs, and said most politely, 'That's all right, mate, we're only rehearsing for tonight.'

The Impersonator enabled me to work with some charming and gifted artistes, notably Jane Griffiths, who played the young school-teacher involved with the boy of the story; an American actor called John Crawford, who was excellent as the USAF officer wrongly accused of the murder; Patricia Burke, who followed a brilliant singing career in musicals with an equally fine career as a straight actress; and John Salew, who brought to life my slimy, bald-headed and sinister comedian. John had once played a dame somewhere, so he knew a lot of tricks and gave a marvellous performance. I was very shocked and sad when he died of a heart attack soon afterwards. I believe *The Impersonator* was his last film.

The key part of the small boy was played by an eight-year-old prodigy called John Dare. He never dried or fluffed once in the course of a long speaking part, in which he had to cry, be angry, sulk, laugh, everything. A remarkable child. One day, we did a shot in which he had to climb down from his chair in the kitchen and run to look out of the window. I said 'Action' and we all stood quiet, holding our breath; the camera was turning, everything was going well. John looked up as directed, reacted to a noise outside, climbed down from his chair, started for the window, then suddenly looked over to me and shouted 'Cut!' Instinctively, we cut. The camera and sound stopped. I said, 'Cut.'

'What did you do that for, Johnnie?' I asked my juvenile star.

'I got off my chair on the wrong side, sir,' he said. 'You told me to get off it on the right-hand side.' I had said so but it didn't matter. We were in a long shot. Perhaps John Dare is by now directing his own pictures with the same meticulous eye for detail.

I was thrilled to get two valuable reviews for *The Impersonator* from Dilys Powell of the *Sunday Times* and Penelope Gilliat of the *Observer*. They both said it was an intelligently made picture of considerable quality and 'with more narrative skill and genuine suspense than many a British thriller made for twice the cost,' or words to that effect. This was just what I had hoped they would say. I have always believed that lavish sets, huge crowds and great stars in expensive costumes are no substitute for originality, visual imagination and a good script. Which brings me to the subject of television and, specifically, television drama, a medium of entertainment which has occupied and absorbed me almost exclusively for the last seven years.

— FIFTEEN —

Electronic Theatre

The first time I ever set foot inside a TV studio was in about 1937 when Edward Cooper, the entertainer at the piano, who was a friend and client of Ellison and Shaughnessy Limited, was booked to appear in a small television variety programme. The BBC were then transmitting in a very experimental way to an incredibly limited viewership from Alexandra Palace. I have an impression of humming electronic equipment and men in white coats moving about the corridors, looking like scientists at some new electrical plant. I also remember Edward Cooper going onto the small set to sit at his piano with an entirely yellow, jaundiced face. Make-up in those early days was stark yellow. One camera trained on Edward as he did his cabaret turn and, of course, he was cued in by a flashing light, exactly as for a live radio broadcast at Portland Place.

After the Second World War, it all took flight at Ally Pally and by the early 'fifties there was a humming drama output, usually on a Sunday night. Most of the plays were old stage and radio successes and they were little more than televised stage productions. Of course, they were rehearsed in outside rehearsal rooms, then brought into the studio as they are today. But the camera techniques were still fairly straightforward and limited by the cameras themselves, their lenses and their lack of mobility.

Many of the early directors of BBC Television were refugees from radio or repertory theatre and found the camera more of a restricting necessity than an instrument for visually artistic presentation. Fred O'Donovan was famous for his refusal to use two cameras. Even his version of Priestley's *The Good Companions*, a major production with crowds, musical numbers and dances, in

135

which Jean appeared, was shot entirely with just one camera. And
I remember Barbara Burnham, who directed my play *Holiday for
Simon* for the BBC Sunday drama slot, whispering to me after the
final run-through in the rehearsal rooms: 'The nice part's over.
Now for those wretched cameras.'

Val Gielgud was Head of Television Drama when my first-ever
full-length play, *Release,* which had been written for the stage but
done twice on radio, was chosen for the Sunday TV play. Michael
Barry had read it and was going to direct, but something cropped
up and it was passed over to Harold Clayton, a very sound, smooth
TV drama director, who always cast his plays very well and never
over-directed his actors.

Release concerned a young woman of twenty-six returning to
her suburban home in South London after serving a 'life' sentence
for murdering her husband. The husband had been affected by the
war and was given to ungovernable tempers and outbursts result-
ing in cruel and sadistic treatment of her. She had been too proud
to admit to her parents that her marriage had failed and had stuck
it out, until one day during a row she smashed a heavy chair on his
head and killed him. When she returns home, after seven years
inside, purged and anxious to begin life anew, her possessive
mother, fearing talk in the neighbourhood if the truth about her
daughter became known, makes a second prison for the girl in her
own home, keeping her indoors and making her ashamed to go out,
and finally tries to undermine a friendship the daughter strikes up
with a man who knows nothing of her past.

This rather meaty part was accepted, to my joy, by Wendy
Hiller and after a nice lunch with Miss Hiller at the Café Royal
rehearsals began. On the second day, Harold Clayton called me in
some distress to say that Wendy Hiller's agent had made a mistake;
she had some days' post-synching to do for a film she'd just finished
and the wretched film people had first call. 'There's nothing we can
do but re-cast.'

The wretched film people proved to be Carol Reed and his
picture *Outcast of the Island* and it was thus that Bill O'Brien, who
was casting director for Korda's London Films, knew of our
problem, felt a bit guilty perhaps and decided to help us out.

'Have you thought of Margaret Leighton?' he said to Harold
Clayton. 'She's free at the moment and hasn't done a television
play.' At that time it was like saying 'Have you thought of Sarah

Bernhardt?' or 'What about Ellen Terry?' Margaret Leighton was the uncrowned queen of the theatre, an actress of immense prestige and glamour. She had worked at the Old Vic with Olivier, Richardson and Guinness and she'd co-starred with Noël Coward, Rex Harrison, everyone of note. When Harold rang me to say she'd agreed to read my play and would I go at once to her flat in Albany and take the script, my heart started thumping uncontrollably.

I was still working at Ealing Studios at the time and I knew that Margaret Leighton had been sent several Ealing scripts in the hope that she would agree to do a film there. Everyone at Ealing, including Mick Balcon, would have given his eye-teeth to get her in a picture. Now I was to persuade her to do my TV play. I rang the bell of her flat and a maid opened the door. She showed me into a neat sitting-room and asked me to wait. I was already an aspiring young French dramatist in the apartment of La Divine Sarah. I clutched my sweaty script and bit my nails. Then Miss Leighton swept in, tall, elegant, graceful, perfumed. She *was* a queen, an empress. She offered me a drink; I asked for a gin and tonic, so she sent her maid across the passage to what she called 'Max's flat' for tonic. She explained that she and her husband, Max Reinhardt, the publisher, found it easier to have a flat each, so as not to disturb each other during the day.

I sipped my gin and tonic and at Miss Leighton's request began to tell her about the play. It was the classic scene of the young author and the great leading lady. The plot sounded awful but I stumbled on and finally left her the script, which she promised, without commitment, to read.

The next day she accepted the part and arrived to join the rest of the cast at rehearsals in Marylebone High Street. Anything less like a suburban girl just out of jug you could not imagine. She came draped in furs, with patent leather court shoes, a huge felt hat, bracelets everywhere, looking just like a film star or a great courtesan.

As rehearsals proceeded, however, Miss Leighton kicked off her high heels and started coming in flat ballet shoes. Next an old jersey and skirt. Then, one day, her hair was straggly and untidy . . . she was becoming Catherine. Suffice it to say that she gave a sensational performance and, since it was her first appearance on television, she attracted a lot of publicity and rave notices. When she won an award for *Release* I felt just a little sour that the play itself had been ignored. But she was sweet and wrote me a charming letter to thank me for a lovely part. That's all we authors really want from actors. Just a gesture of thanks for the words we put into their mouths.

The day after *Release* had been shown on television three film companies made enquiries about the film rights. However, the reaction that pleased me most was a letter from Sir Barry Jackson of the famous Birmingham Repertory Theatre asking to read the script. The upshot was that *Release,* beautifully directed by Douglas Seale, and with a cast including Rosalind Boxall, Alfred Burke and Paul Daneman, opened the 1951 autumn season at Birmingham. The local press notices and that of *The Times* were virtual raves and I was hailed as a brilliant young (I was thirty-five!) playwright with a great future.

After *Release* I wrote a gentle romantic comedy for the stage, *Holiday For Simon,* and that too was televised. In 1953 I joined the BBC for one year at Lime Grove as a resident adaptor and script editor. This job, which involved working with Giles Cooper and Nigel Kneale among others, consisted of reading and reporting on plays sent in for consideration; cutting and adapting stage plays for television production; cutting and adapting classics (I once had to take twenty minutes out of Ibsen's *Lady from the Sea* and you can't cut Ibsen) and at one point writing to order a six-part thriller serial for Saturday night.

The serial was to follow Nigel Kneale's *Quatermass Experiment* which had gripped the entire nation by the throat. It was an impossible job, of course, but at least the success of *Quatermass* had built up a big audience for the Saturday night thriller. I wrote a serial called *A Place of Execution.* It was about the daughter of a British Governor of a colony in the Middle East, who is kidnapped in London and held hostage against the hanging by her father of a terrorist. I called my fictitious country Zirdanah, the terrorist organization 'Kailak' and the Governor, Sir John Harper.

A few years later EOKA emerged in Cyprus, where Sir John Harding was Governor and a British soldier was kidnapped as hostage against the execution of one of their terrorist leaders. Either I have second sight or Colonel Grivas saw *A Place of Execution* and copied my plot.

All six episodes of my serial were directed by a young Canadian, Alvin Rakoff, who soon went on most deservedly to bigger and better things.

Incidentally TV history was made on *A Place of Execution,* for in the final episode we cross-cut scenes in the studio at Ally Pally with scenes recorded live on location in the Chamber of Horrors at Madame Tussaud's. It was the first time in a TV drama production that live Outside Broadcast scenes were piped through GPO lines into a drama studio to cue in with studio scenes, all live. Because the terrorists almost succeeded in hanging Miss Caroline Harper from the old gallows in the Chamber of Horrors, the press made quite a big sensation of the denouement. *The News of the World* headline on Sunday morning screamed 'Millions See Girl Hanged' and I was castigated by the critics for writing an unsavoury, sadistic, blood-thirsty serial. Today it would only cause toddlers in a playschool to yawn with boredom.

Another highlight of my year with the BBC was *Our Marie.* Michael Mills, a brilliant, whizzy producer, was doing a series of big, show business, musical biographies called *The Passing Show.* He had done one about George Edwardes and was later to do Vesta Tilley, C. B. Cochran and others. Now a *Passing Show* play about Marie Lloyd was being planned. Michael asked me to write the script; so, in company with Christopher Barry, who did all the research and chased up books, cuttings, records, etc., I proceeded with the mammoth task.

It was a fascinating if arduous undertaking. I had to write imagined scenes between Marie and her family in Hoxton, her agent, her various husbands, her variety managers, all from the basis of what was known of her life and with a surviving sister, Alice, in the background.

A mighty cast of hundreds was assembled round Pat Kirkwood as Marie; there were thirty sets, hundreds of costumes, filmed inserts, a full-scale theatre orchestra, singers, dancers and numerous extras. It was just about the biggest production the BBC had ever undertaken in the Lime Grove Studios and it was all live!

I won't dwell on what happened. It has become TV history and a fuller account of it is given in Peter Bull's highly entertaining autobiography *I Know the Face But. . . .* Suffice it to say that after a horrifying start, when the studio sound went dead seconds after the first bars of the overture, the entire show was stopped for five minutes of light music over a still photograph of a river bend in the Cotswolds and a spoken apology. It then restarted from the opening bars, to run for nearly two hours and was a total triumph of technical skill, energy, cool nerve and sheer guts for Pat Kirkwood, the director, Peter Graham Scott, and the studio crew.

Pat was magnificent. She dashed about from set to set, stripping as she ran, pursued by wardrobe girls throwing her next dress over her head; she arrived on cue for her next song in the next setting, be it a café, a music publisher's office, her home or a variety stage; she sang the numbers with zest and charm, accompanied by Eric Robinson and the orchestra, who were in a different studio keeping time with her through headphones; she never put a foot wrong.

She arrived, concealing breathless anxiety, on the different sets, always in the right dress and wig, although those responsible for dressing her had often lost the place. Here she would encounter other actors and actresses ready to play their scenes with her, their faces betraying ill-concealed relief to see her actually *there*. In spite of the panic Pat spoke every word of her dialogue correctly, never so much as a syllable out of place. This is a rare achievement in TV which will always endear any artiste to any author. The whole thing was a nightmare but Pat got through somehow and, as the last chorus of 'My Old Man' reached its climax and held until the green light went on and the show was over, the whole cast, every technician in the studio and the entire orchestra and chorus, who came running in from the next stage, broke out into a thunder of spontaneous applause and cheers for Pat Kirkwood.

Soon after the TV show, I was invited to lunch at the Carlton with Jack Hylton and Pat to discuss a stage musical version of *Our Marie*. I was thrilled at the prospect of adapting my television script into a libretto for a theatre musical at Drury Lane or His Majesty's. Over lunch we debated the project in detail. Pat wanted desperately to do it and was trying to persuade Jack Hylton to agree. He seemed enthusiastic enough when we parted. I waited for a call to start writing but it never came. Jack Hylton had gone cold on the idea. I was sad. More than anything, I'd have loved the chance to work with Pat again.

After my year as a script editor I drifted back into films for some years and it was not until 1964 that I returned to TV for regular employment.

I had written several odd one-off plays for television including two 'Love Story' plays for ATV and I'd had a short spell under contract to Rediffusion as a sort of resident playwright. One contribution to Rediffusion at this time was a play called *Breaking Point* in which the talented Sian Phillips co-starred with Griffith Jones. It was a simple, quite moving little 'triangle' play about the end of a love affair between a married man and his secretary – very 'Peg's Paper', I suppose, which is why it topped the ratings.

Some years later this piece was published by the English Theatre Guild as a 'double bill' with *The Tea Cosy,* a black comedy I had written some time before for the BBC. These two one-acters fared extremely well with the reps and amateurs. So my agent arranged with an Austrian play publisher not only a German version but a staging of the two plays in Vienna. The production, entitled *Gäste Zum Tee* (Guests for Tea), was scheduled for the day after Christmas at the Theater der Courage. Thrilled beyond measure and imagining a glittering first night in some plush-and-gilt rococo playhouse of Habsburg days, with chandeliers and boxes filled with all the beautiful women of Vienna, I boarded an Austrian Airlines Caravelle at Heathrow and settled in my seat. A pretty stewardess came down the aisle selling copies of the *Wiener Tageblatt.* I bought one, opened it, and saw my photograph prominently displayed on the arts page with a write-up about my plays. My pride knew no bounds. I was Ibsen himself on his way to a production of *The Master Builder* in Berlin.

We landed at the Schwechat Airport in deep snow. Christmas in Vienna – romance, excitement. At the hotel I was interviewed for the radio. What was my opinion of English drama? What did I think of Osborne, Wesker, Whiting? I had a bath and changed. The translator of the plays came to take me to the Theater der Courage. We drove in a taxi along the Franz Josef's Kai and stopped by the entrance of what looked like a small shop. We got out, and went down some stone steps; a slight smell of cheroots and paint; then a tiny room with a little stage at one end; faded, shabby drapes. The room was full of people, sitting on hard chairs: most were scruffy and bearded, some looked like university professors; all the Vienna critics were there.

The evening was a total disaster. The audience had come to see a pair of avante-garde experimental plays by a new English dramatist. What they got was a couple of terribly simple entertainments written for television, one a black comedy about a Kensington teashop and a body in a trunk, the other this straight play about the end of an affair. I was crucified by most of the critics, one notice describing the evening as 'A Cup of Weak English Tea'. Only the critic from Linz was kind. *'Ein erfolgreicher Abend'*, he said. Bless him. I flew back in a blizzard, low and depressed, masochistically translating my awful notices with the help of a pocket dictionary and wishing I'd never learnt the wretched language.

In 1964 something of great importance happened to me. I was summoned to see Stella Richman, the very shrewd and talented ex-actress who was executive producer in charge of drama series at Rediffusion. Under her aegis, John Whitney was script-editing a very hot, fast-moving underworld series, *The Informer*, which had Ian Hendry in the role of a dis-barred barrister turned police informer. It was about to go into a second series. Stella was empire-building and ready to hand over the day-to-day production of *The Informer* to Whitney. This meant finding a new script-editor. I was invited to take over the scripts and much of the writing of *The Informer* and from that day to this I have been script-editing and writing for TV series non-stop. For this is my niche; what I believe I can do best. After years of writing, producing, directing and working with good writers, and having a fertile imagination plus some technical knowledge of dramatic story-telling, I felt ready to opt for the rather ghostly, backroom task of preparing and often secretly doctoring series scripts. I saw it as a profession that might keep me working into my old age. I hope so. At any rate I am indebted forever to Stella Richman and John Whitney for giving me the start to a new career.

After *The Informer* I edited and wrote for another series for Rediffusion about nuns in a convent, called *Sanctuary*. This presented problems for we had three elderly leading ladies, Fay Compton, Alison Leggatt and Peggy Thorpe-Bates, and a younger one, Joanna Dunham. Each kept a beady eye on the length of the others' parts from week to week; each needed tactful handling. As a Catholic myself, who had received instruction in a convent in my youth, I knew the score and in the second series, the one I edited, we had some pretty hard-hitting stories and with John Harrison, a theatre man of great artistic integrity and imagination, producing, we got the nuns into the ratings.

At Yorkshire Television I launched the first series of *Hadleigh*, starring Gerald Harper, which was a spin-off from a local newspaper series called 'Gazette'.

Then Stella Richman summoned me back to what had become

London Weekend TV (a newly franchised descendant of Rediffusion) to take over again for the second half of a wartime Resis-
tance series, *Manhunt*. Again the script editor, Andrew Brown,
was stepping up to produce and I came into his place and saw
Manhunt through to the end.

— SIXTEEN —

Upstairs, Downstairs and Elsewhere

If a man is going to succeed in his career or reach a point of self-fulfilment, I'm certain it is better to do so later in life rather than earlier. The world of sport and entertainment is littered with tragic cases of young men and women who have achieved spectacular success and fame before the age of thirty, lacked the character or wisdom not to be spoilt by early success, failed to sustain the high level of output expected of them and slipped away into embittered oblivion.

I was lucky. I hit a mild form of fame and success at the age of fifty-six and if I am to slip into oblivion, it won't be embittered for I've had it good for a long time, my journey to success was up a gradual incline over the years, rather than a spectacular leap to the summit in youth. I became script editor and began to write scripts for the London Weekend Television series *Upstairs, Downstairs* when I was fifty-three and this chapter in my writing career lifted me up onto my own personal peak as regards fame and money at a mercifully mature age.

Upstairs, Downstairs began with two actresses getting an idea while swimming in a pool in the South of France and ended with 300 million people sitting glued to their TV sets all over the world from Los Angeles to Sydney, from Paris to Saudi Arabia . . . holding their breath, as the fortunes of the Bellamy family and their servants unfolded before their sore eyes. My part in this saga can be outlined briefly. As related previously, I had become a sort of doyen of series editors. Around this time two old friends of mine approached me, John Hawkesworth, a TV producer with whom I had served both in the Grenadier Guards in the war and later in the Rank Organization at Pinewood Studios, and John Whitney, who had produced *The Informer*. They had formed Sagitta Productions Limited, a concern for finding good format ideas for TV and radio programmes, packaging them and presenting them to the companies.

To them had come actress Jean Marsh, with whom Whitney and I had worked on *The Informer,* together with her close friend, actress Eileen Atkins, both bubbling over with an idea for a comedy series for themselves to appear in. The two girls had been staying at the charming villa in the Alpes Maritimes owned by Paddy and Vivienne Glenavy (he being Paddy Campbell of the *Sunday Times* and the engaging stammer) when they had come up with the idea of a TV comedy series about two maids in a Victorian country house – falling up the stairs with laden trays, and into the hay with lecherous footmen and all that kind of thing. It was to be called 'Below Stairs'. The two Johns, who are nothing if not shrewd showmen, instantly realized that the subject of domestic servants in a big house had never been treated dramatically on TV, but they felt the house should be an Edwardian London mansion and the series should be as much about an MP and his family as about the domestic servants below stairs in the servants' hall.

So Hawkesworth and Whitney created the 'original' Bellamy family: Richard Bellamy, MP, his wife, Gail, an ex-actress, and Bellamy's son and daughter, James and Elizabeth, by his divorced first wife. There was a butler, Frank Hudson; a cook, Mrs Bridges; and various unspecified servants, including the two funny maids. 'Below Stairs' was packaged up, and the new format was written and presented by Sagitta Productions to Stella Richman, then Controller of Programmes at London Weekend Television. Apart from Jean and Eileen as the two maids, the package included me as script editor, to take over as soon as I was finished on *Manhunt*.

We had a number of meetings at this stage and John Hawkesworth and I discussed the series in some detail. The Bellamy house was to be in Regent's Park, so I took John off to look at a fine house in Cumberland Terrace which belonged to my friends Paul and Gabby Bowman. It had a quiet private road approach and seemed an ideal location. At this stage I also wrote a memo in which I suggested that Richard Bellamy should be – like Duff Cooper – a brilliant, Foreign Office-trained son of a Norfolk parson, who had married into one of the great landed families. I created the character of Lady Marjorie Talbot-Carey, daughter of the Earl of Southwold, a former Prime Minister (loosely based on Lord Salisbury) for Bellamy's wife, who would entertain for him lavishly and generally steer him towards Downing Street.

It seemed to me that this set-up, so familiar in British politics, would give us possible conflict in the family: Bellamy, a Tory by marriage with slight liberal leanings, under the patronage as a son-in-law of a powerful political family. There would be echoes of Harold Macmillan and Lady Dorothy Cavendish, Mr Ormsby-Gore and Lady Beatrice Cecil and, of course, Duff Cooper and Lady Diana Manners. It also lifted the Bellamys in the social scale and gave us the chance to fill the house with smart people, including King Edward himself.

At this point Stella Richman sent for John Hawkesworth and me and told us to start the script operation at once. Sagitta generously gave the two actresses fifty per cent of all the earnings of the series, whose title was swiftly and wisely changed to *Upstairs, Downstairs* after someone had pointed out that Margaret Powell had recently published a book called *Below Stairs* about her life as a kitchen maid in the 'twenties.

Over the next four years John Hawkesworth and I worked very hard and very closely as a team. As each series began, we sat down and discussed the general direction of the stories and the historical background to the years we were to cover. We both came up with ideas for episodes; I then wrote down the outline in detail, scenes and situations, for every episode and briefed each writer accordingly. So the wheels began to turn.

Gordon Jackson, to the eternal credit of Martin Case, the imaginative casting director, was engaged to play Hudson, who duly became a Scots butler and caused me to change his first name from Frank to Angus. I suggested Rachel Gurney, an old friend who had appeared in my TV play *Holiday for Simon* and a film I once made, *Room in the House,* for the part of Lady Marjorie and was more than pleased when, after taking her to meet John over coffee at his flat, the latter agreed to cast her.

What followed over the next four or five years has become TV history. Suffice it to say that all of us engaged on the project – actors, actresses, designers, producer, directors, writers – combined to provide the world with something that became almost a cult, a way of life in over thirty-six countries and in the process, I think, we all had a ball. Every moment of making 'Updown', as we tended to call it, was a joy and a thrill.

I personally received and still receive letters from all over the world praising our efforts, many of them from old friends and acquaintances, people from my schooldays, from the war, people from childhood, long since forgotten. I even had one or two letters from former servants, who had been with us at Norfolk Square and St James's saying how nostalgic the series was, evoking the good old days of the servants' hall.

One old lady in Nuneaton wrote to London Weekend to say her butler was retiring and would Hudson be free to come for an interview. Our characters really existed for some people beyond the suspension of disbelief.

I think those characters were also pretty real to the actors, although they were not always loved by their interpreters. Gordon Jackson detested Hudson, the butler, whom he found – and rightly – to be a two-faced, pompous prig. The nicest characteristic Hudson possessed was that he was a football fan. In 1930 my brother Tom and I were taken to the Cup Final at Wembley by our family butler, Jones. Joey had some extra tickets given to him and, as he was himself going in the Royal Box with the Prince of Wales, we got them. So Tom and I were taken off by Tube to see Arsenal beat Huddersfield 2-1 in the charge of this bowler-hatted butler. That incident prompted me to make Hudson a Chelsea supporter.

When in the Great War series, we decided that James Bellamy should be awarded the MC, we didn't tell Simon Williams in advance but allowed him to discover the fact in the relevant script when it arrived at his home by the post a week or so before rehearsals for the episode. There was a distinct gleam of pride in Simon's eye when he turned up at the read-through to be congratulated by the assembled cast. John Hawkesworth and I almost felt we should have staged an investiture for him in the rehearsal rooms.

Likewise, David Langton seemed to gain stature when I created Richard Bellamy, then Civil Lord of the Admiralty, a Viscount in Episode Nine of Series Four. To help make his elevation to the House of Lords as realistic as possible, I caused Bellamy, who was noted for his impeccable manners, to receive a telegram of congratulation on New Year's morning, 1916, from his old friend and colleague, Lord Curzon of Kedleston. This, as was his wont, Curzon had couched in verse:

> Dear courteous Commoner, whose loss the Lower House
>   can ill afford,
> Hail, friend, the Upper House has gained a Civil Lord.

I was rather pleased with that, though Curzon himself might
have thought it a trifle facile.

Apart from controlling and co-ordinating the development and
destinies of the characters and dreaming up story ideas and situations for them, a script editor on a series must also at times arrange
to 'write out' of the series characters whose players must for some
reason leave the cast. It has become a tradition that in such events
the character is either sent off abroad or allowed to die, or both. I
was obliged to fulfil this awful duty of what I now call 'character
assassination' on two occasions in 'Updown'; first on dear Rachel
Gurney, who wished to leave after Series Two but agreed to appear
in Episode One of Series Three; and second on Meg Wynn Owen,
who played James's wife, Hazel.

When Rachel told John and me at lunch in a Chelsea restaurant
that she wanted to go but would do the first episode of Series Three,
we were sad but had to agree. John suggested a hunting accident,
being himself a keen follower of the Cottesmore Hounds, but we'd
never really established Lady Marjorie as a hunting lady. I went
away to have a think and it came to me in a flash that the year in
question was 1912. Having been at Pinewood when Roy Baker was
making the film *A Night to Remember* and having also sat stunned
in my seat at the age of fifteen watching Noël Coward's immortal
show *Cavalcade* at Drury Lane with its poignant *Titanic* scene,
a little bird in my brain said to me *'Titanic'* and I wrote an end
scene to Episode One, revealing at the last moment that her lady-
ship had sailed for America in that ill-fated ship. It was a dignified
and appropriate death for Lady Marjorie I thought, although
some critics considered my 'coup' a bit facile.

Poor Hazel Bellamy had to be removed as a character at the end
of Series Four, so again I went off to have a think. It was 1918,
Armistice Year, and I suddenly remembered the terrible irony of
the flu epidemic that had killed off millions who had come through
the war itself unscathed. So Hazel died of Spanish flu.

When Nicola Pagett wanted out as Elizabeth, the Bellamy
daughter, we were all very sad, for she is a fine actress and had done
us proud. But I couldn't help agreeing with her reasons for going.

She felt Elizabeth had done everything possible as a character and could only become static in future. She had rebelled against her parents; run away from a ball at Londonderry House; married an effeminate poet; suffered sexual frustration through a non-consummated marriage; slept with her husband's publisher; got an annulment to her marriage only to become pregnant; had her illegitimate baby; left her husband; taken up with an Armenian millionaire; dragged Rose, the housemaid, with her into a Suffragette raid; got caught and sent to Holloway; and quarrelled with her father, her mother and her brother, whilst being on dangerously familiar terms with the servants. What more could Elizabeth do but sail for America with her love child and marry a well-to-do New York lawyer called Dana?

Inevitably the day-to-day task of editing the scripts for *Upstairs, Downstairs* involved a great deal of time-consuming but often highly rewarding research. Dates and facts had to be looked up in endless books borrowed from the London Library; old newspapers were scanned at Colindale; costumes and props were examined at the Victoria and Albert Museum and elsewhere. One day I would be at Wetherby's searching through the *Racing Calendar* of 1919 to find out which horse had won the Ascot Gold Cup that year; another day would find me telephoning the Royal Aero Club to ask the secretary how much James Bellamy would have paid in 1922 for an old wartime Avro 504K; a flip through back numbers of Hansard was occasionally undertaken to discover what was being debated in the Commons – or more often the Lords – on a certain afternoon, so that Lord Bellamy could comment on the matter at dinner.

One very joyous morning I left the Imperial War Museum wreathed in smiles. I had decided to open the post-Great War series in the summer of 1919 with the very distant sound of bands playing, enabling Hudson in the servant's hall to mention the Victory Parade which would have been – so I thought – just audible from 165 Eaton Place as it rounded Hyde Park Corner. At the museum I had looked up the actual route taken by the vast parade of Allied troops on Saturday, July 19th, 1919, Peace Day. I could hardly believe my luck when I discovered that the procession had marched up Sloane Street, through Pont Street into Belgrave Square, then turned right out of Belgrave Square, crossing Eaton Place en route for Victoria. This fact gave me a whole scene in my script – the excited young maids and the footman getting Hudson's permission to race down the street to the corner of Eaton Place to see the procession, including James and Georgina, march by, while Hudson and Mrs Bridges watched it from the first-floor balcony through a deerstalking telescope passed on to Hudson by his father, a gillie in Aberdeenshire.

Upstairs, Downstairs was produced, for all its seemingly costly period settings and costumes, on a surprisingly modest budget. The challenge was to create the atmosphere outside the house in Eaton Place through the dialogue – as on the stage. To go out with film or electronic cameras and shoot exterior scenes is very expensive and the action must justify the cost. Apart from a few discreet shots of ancient motorcars driving about, we did manage three major 'locations'.

The first was a trip with the cast to Herne Bay to record an August Bank Holiday outing on the eve of the outbreak of the Great War, when the Bellamy servants bathed in the sea and picnicked. Another pair of scripts took James and Hazel to the Newburys' stately home, Somerby, represented by Burley-on-the-Hill, a large, elegant house near Oakham owned by friends and neighbours of John Hawkesworth. On the first occasion John set up a magnificent hunting sequence with the Cottesmore Hounds, and later a shooting party in the surrounding woods.

Perhaps the most ambitious piece of exterior recording occurred one Sunday, when we took over Marylebone Station for the day with a train made up of 1916 rolling stock borrowed from the Railway Museum. We also had several old buses, cars and lorries and a large crowd of extras. We were filming a scene showing the departure of a troop train to the front, and the arrival of a hospital train back from the front. A troop train, packed with soldiers, had to steam out of the station on our left, the crowds waving goodbye to the departing soldiers; then into the opposite platform, seen to our right, was to steam a hospital train filled with wounded soldiers, nurses and stretcher bearers.

In between the departure of the troop train and the arrival of the hospital train we were able to cut to a shot of Georgina and her friend talking on the platform to some subalterns. It was just as well we could. For, owing to a shortage of period coaches, the departing troop train was painted white on its far, invisible side, and on the white were painted large red crosses.As soon as the train was clear of the station and had halted beyond the points, make-up girls, hidden from view when the train left, transformed the previously immaculate and healthy soldiers into sick and bloody men. We recorded our platform scenes and then, right on cue, the train returned, its reverse side now displaying the red crosses, and its occupants crippled, maimed and bloody as they were helped out onto the platform.

During one take of the arrival of the hospital train, a lady about to leave from an adjacent platform to visit her sister in Rickmansworth caught sight from her compartment of our trainload of wounded soldiers, thought that they had just arrived back from Northern Ireland and ran to offer assistance with the mobile canteen.

That lady's emotional response to the sight of the hospital train was precisely that of Georgina Worsley, Richard Bellamy's young ward. Misty-eyed at the sight of such suffering she too rushes off to help in a canteen and ultimately to enrol as a nurse. The part of Georgina was played by the stunningly beautiful Lesley-Anne Down, with whom male viewers fell in love by the thousand.

One continual problem, when one is striving for period accuracy, is the use of idiom in dialogue. Sometimes it's easy. You know for sure that English people in the 'thirties spoke of going for a 'bathe' and not for a 'swim' which was then an Americanism; that modern phrases such as 'not to worry', 'you've got to be joking' and 'let's get it together' were not to be heard in Edwardian drawing-rooms. It's the subtler things that may cause trouble. My rule is, if in doubt don't use it or you'll distract the viewer. Let me give an example. In one episode of *Upstairs, Downstairs,* set in 1905 or thereabouts, the scriptwriters Terence Brady and Charlotte Bingham referred to 'cocktails'. My pencil went straight through the word, which I amended to 'champagne'. The Bradys, however, had checked up and found that, in some fairly smart and sophisticated London homes in 1905, the cocktail had already arrived from America. Nevertheless I knew that the use of the word in that period would provoke telephone calls from viewers and the outbreak of heated arguments in the living-rooms of many homes, events which can disturb and even destroy the viewing of a programme. The Bradys were perfectly correct but they saw my point and agreed to the change.

At one stage during the production of *Upstairs, Downstairs* I

became entangled quite amicably with John Freeman, London
Weekend Television's Chief Executive and thus my boss. I had
written a scene wherein Lady Marjorie ordered Hudson to 'leave
the sweet on the sideboard'. It was set in 1910 or 1911. John Freeman wrote a memo pointing out that 'sweet' was a middle-class
term for what some still call 'dessert', others 'pudding', and a few
'afters'. I had formed the impression that 'sweet' was the original
upper-class word, which like certain other words such as 'serviette',
'toilet' and 'settee' had slipped down from above into middle-class
usage later on. I felt quite sure I could remember my mother, who
would not have erred, discussing with our cook in the 1920s what
to have for a 'sweet'. My belief was that 'sweet' was taken up by
the bourgeoisie just before or during World War II and immortal-
ized as a middle-class term by John Betjeman – 'Is trifle sufficient
for sweet?' And that it was this that pushed the U-people into
talking of 'pudding'. John Freeman and I exchanged a couple
of memos on the subject and to this day I am not sure who was
right.

Another minefield for the unwary or unversed scriptwriter was
the method of address used between servants and family and
certain other rules concerning titles. For example, much time was
spent by me trying to explain the seemingly nonsensical fact that
whereas Rose, the head housemaid, would call the butler 'Mr
Hudson' to his face or to another servant, she would refer to him
to any member of the family or to visitors as 'Hudson'. Similarly
the only members of the family who could ever speak of 'Mr
Hudson' would be the children, but they, nevertheless, would call
Rose 'Rose' and not 'Miss Buck'. It took time too to get some of the
writers out of the habit of having Hudson say, 'Yes, all right, your
lordship' in response to an order from Bellamy, instead of the
correct: 'Very good, m'lord.'

Another trap for those unversed in the strange ways of *Debrett*
was the use of courtesy titles as opposed to hereditary ones. In the
early episodes of the series there were those, including some of the
press, who felt that if the mistress of the house was Lady Marjorie
Bellamy, her husband *must* be Lord Bellamy. Conversely, some
writers called her Lady Bellamy, while Richard was still an esquire
and not yet a peer.

Our major problem was that in order to get the detail right, we
were forced to appear the most appalling snobs. It was sometimes

necessary to correct mispronunciation, for example, which would have jarred on certain viewers and undermined their belief in the breeding and background of the character concerned. All young actors and actresses today pronounce their 'a' sounds as 'u', in order to get as far away as possible from the toffee-nosed, upper-crust, pinched 'a' sound. They will speak of an 'upsolutely funtustic mun'. It may sometimes be a North Country accent coming through, but I believe it is a retreat from 'ayabsolootly fayantay-istic mayan'.

There were times too when players depicting the upper classes had to be instructed not to say 'host*ess*', or Asc*ot*', or 'pardon' and 'have a sherry'.

Richard Bellamy's grandson today would probably play lead guitar in a rock group or manage a launderette in the Fulham Road. His granddaughter might be in Holloway for drug offences or running a sandwich bar in Sloane Square. Their dialogue would present no special problems for a script editor. Both would speak in the tongue of the common man, their sentences punctuated with those overworked monosyllables 'yeah' and 'great' and the tri-syllable 'amazing'. And their costumes would be a walk-over for the wardrobe supervisors: both would wear sweater and jeans. Some of their friends would be sharing a basement flat in 165 Eaton Place; the old servants' hall would be their living-room, its walls bearing posters of Kitchener pointing as he pointed at Edward, the footman, sixty years ago. And up in the attic, in Ruby's room or Rose's, would be a tiny flat shared by Lady Prudence's granddaughter Caroline, a drama student at Central, with her best friend in her year, Carol, whose grandmother was in service most of her life next door at 167 Eaton Place and knew Mrs Bridges quite well.

Although London Weekend Television would have liked to continue the Bellamy saga well beyond 1930, the year of Georgina Worsley's marriage to Lord Stockbridge, we all felt that it was time to stop. We'd come a long way from the original idea of life in a grand Edwardian London house, reflecting the grace and elegance of that age. By taking the Bellamys through twenty-eight years of British history we were already cheating on their ages. Richard had been a mature MP in his fifties in 1902 and would by 1930 be a man in his late seventies; Hudson would be almost an octogenar-ian. But they were not made-up or bewigged for senility and the viewers were becoming aware of the deception. Georgina had nursed in the war, yet in 1930 she was still a flapper in her twenties. It was indeed time to stop.

We all received many compliments over the course of five series but I must record two of very special importance that were paid to me. One was the decision to show my episode 'Guest of Honour' about King Edward's visit to dine and play bridge at the Bellamy home as a special piece of TV drama outside the competition but on a vast screen to a packed audience at the 1975 Prix Italia Festival in Florence. The other was the decision of the *New Yorker* television critic, Michael J. Arlen, to print in his review a whole scene from one of my scripts, 'Miss Forrest', to illustrate the quality of the writing on the series. That same episode, incidentally, won me one of my two Hollywood Emmy nominations for writing, so I suppose that must be my third major compliment.

Anyway, it's all over now and we are left with press cuttings and happy memories of – for me – a great, unrepeatable triumph in what is sometimes called 'the afternoon of my life'. That brings me back to my opening remarks about success in early age. *Upstairs, Downstairs* hasn't spoiled me. I'm too damn old now.

I followed *Upstairs, Downstairs* with *The Cedar Tree,* a modestly budgeted family saga of my own invention for ATV. It is the story of a former Naval Commander and his wife bringing up their three daughters in an old Georgian house in Herefordshire between 1934 and 1939. It is drawn absolutely from life. I stayed in many such houses in my youth. And it all seems like yesterday.

—— SEVENTEEN ——

Reflections

Looking back on my strangely mixed life, hovering awkwardly between high society and show business, I suppose it can best be symbolized by a certain evening at St James's in 1949, when my mother was away in America.

Joey had always admired Gertrude Lawrence and had met her once or twice. She was in London at the time appearing in Daphne du Maurier's play *September Tide* and Joey had decided to give a party for her one night after the show. One day he telephoned me and Jean at our flat in Chesham Street and gave us orders to appear at St James's the following evening at about 10 p.m. Black tie. Not to be late. I was thrilled at the chance to meet Gertie Lawrence and gathered that it was to be quite a small supper party. The other guests were to include Daphne du Maurier herself, her husband, General 'Boy' Browning, and Carroll Gibbons was coming along to play the piano. Obliging on the keys was usually my role at informal parties, so I thought to myself: 'That's my lot. No piano for me tonight.' Anyway, Gertie arrived from the theatre and we all had supper, delicious cold food and champagne. We danced and sang old numbers, until Joey suddenly asked us all to pause for a moment. The front-door bell had rung and Joey went down to the hall, returning with one of his splendid mischievous grins all over his face, accompanied by Princess Elizabeth and Prince Philip. It was his surprise for Gertie. The party continued and some of us did turns.

When towards midnight Carroll had to leave to fulfil his contract at the Savoy Hotel, the old family Bluthner, which I knew so well, fell vacant. I was persuaded – very nervous, for once – to play. I started off my act, as I often do, with 'Mrs Worthington'.

That went all right. Then I played 'Where or When?' for dancing. Finally I took a deep breath and risked my neck. I turned to Miss Lawrence as she floated by, murmured, 'Hope you don't mind,' and started to play very softly 'Someone to Watch Over Me' by Gershwin. And, guess what? That divine, incomparable, heavenly woman started to sing it, so softly and so sweetly off-key on the high notes. She stopped dancing, stood beside me and sang it and I played for her and bells were ringing in my ears. Then we did 'Some Day I'll Find You' from *Private Lives*. I was in heaven. Me accompanying Gertrude Lawrence on the old family Bluthner grand, the one on which I'd picked out 'Tea for Two' with one finger as a child at Norfolk Square and composed some of my own numbers. Our piano. I shall never forget *that* evening as long as I live.

In October 1955 my mother died in her bedroom upstairs in that gracious house and our family connection with St James's came to an end. Joey had died only hours before in Sister Agnes' Home.

The last days at St James's Palace were a sort of blurred nightmare. I remember the funeral service for them both in the Chapel Royal and the long hours spent sorting out their papers and belongings, furniture to be sold, probate, letters of condolence to be answered and countless other duties to be performed.

The house was handed over in due course to Lord Scarborough, who with Lady Scarborough mercifully took over much of the carpeting and curtaining. The Scarboroughs were kindness itself and made the task of getting out so much easier than it might have been. The house has since accommodated Lord Cobbold and Lord MacLean, so it seems to have become once and for all the official residence of the Lord Chamberlain.

It is a curious sensation to approach the age at which one's parents died. A slight shudder goes through you at the thought that you are getting on. It makes a man retrospective and, as in my case, prompts the desire to 'sign the Visitors' Book of Life before leaving', if only for the possible amusement and interest of one's descendants.

I am blessed with two witty, talented and attractive sons and I have written this book mainly for them, their mother and their children. But it doesn't mean that I am finished, with nothing left to do. Somerset Maugham outlived his *The Summing Up*, with all its sombre finality, by a quarter of a century. So let us not be downhearted. It is not the end, yet, I hope.

— APPENDIX —

Dramatic Works by the Author

STAGE PLAYS
Release
The Tea-Cosy
Holiday for Simon
Breaking Point
Light Fingers
Serenita
The Heat of the Moment
Never Walk Alone

FILM SCRIPTS
Brandy for the Parson
Laxdale Hall
Room in the House
Just My Luck
A Touch of the Sun
The Hostage
Follow That Horse
The Impersonator
Crescendo
The Flesh and Blood Show
Tiffany Jones
The High Terrace

TELEVISION PLAYS
The Small Hours
Sweet Sorrow
What's the Matter, Darling? Can't You Sleep?
Our Marie

RADIO PLAY
The Cost of a Conscience

TELEVISION SERIES (CONTRIBUTED TO)
A Place of Execution
The Informer
Sanctuary
Hadleigh
Manhunt
The Saint
Spyder's Web
Upstairs, Downstairs
The Cedar Tree

FILMS DIRECTED
Suspended Alibi
Cat Girl
Six-Five Special
The Impersonator

FILMS PRODUCED
Brandy for the Parson
Laxdale Hall
The End of the Road
Room in the House
Heart of a Child

INDEX

161